*Surviving the Apocalypse*
*in the Suburbs*

This is a clear-eyed, straight-ahead manual for what's shaping up to be permanent hard times. The long-term destiny of suburbia may be a dark passage, but for quite a while ahead a lot of normal people will be living there, and they would do well to prepare themselves with this book.

—James Howard Kunstler, author *The Long Emergency*
and the *World Made By Hand* novels

Problematic as suburbia will inevitably become in the dawning age of limits, around a third of the people of North America live there, and economic contraction and imploding real estate markets will keep a good many of them there for the foreseeable future. In this eminently practical and thoughtful book, Wendy Brown takes on the challenge of exploring the options for surviving and thriving through hard times in the suburbs, and carries it off with aplomb. Highly recommended.

—John Michael Greer, author *The Long Descent*
and the weekly blog *The Archdruid Report*
www.thearchdruidreport.blogspot.com

A real treasure amidst the gloom and doom, this comes like a breath of fresh air. It paints an optimistic yet sober and realistic picture of how those living in the suburbs could become self-sufficient in the inevitable post-petroleum age. Those who plan can thrive and lead a meaningful, deeply satisfying, full life. Everything you need to know about preparing to live off the grid in 21 days is here in this riveting, deeply insightful, clear headed, highly original, and richly informed guide. Beautifully written and full of wisdom, it is a great read with an eye to important details.

—Connie Bright (Krochmal), author *Making It: An Encyclopedia of How to Do It for Less*, and Master Gardener, Burpee Seeds

# SURVIVING
## THE APOCALYPSE
# IN THE SUBURBS

## THE THRIVALIST'S GUIDE
## TO LIFE WITHOUT OIL

**WENDY BROWN**

NEW SOCIETY PUBLISHERS

Cover design by Diane McIntosh.
All photos © iStock (picmax)

Printed in Canada. First printing March 2011.

ISBN 978-0-86571-681-0    eISBN 978-1-55092-471-8

Inquiries regarding requests to reprint all or part of
*Surviving the Apocalypse in the Suburbs* should be addressed to
New Society Publishers at the address below.

To order directly from the publishers, please call toll-free (North America)
1-800-567-6772, or order online at www.newsociety.com

Any other inquiries can be directed by mail to:
New Society Publishers
P.O. Box 189, Gabriola Island, BC V0R 1X0, Canada
(250) 247-9737

New Society Publishers' mission is to publish books that contribute in fundamental
ways to building an ecologically sustainable and just society, and to do so with the
least possible impact on the environment, in a manner that models this vision. We
are committed to doing this not just through education, but through action. Our
printed, bound books are printed on Forest Stewardship Council-certified acid-
free paper that is **100% post-consumer recycled** (100% old growth forest-free),
processed chlorine free, and printed with vegetable-based, low-VOC inks, with
covers produced using FSC-certified stock. New Society also works to reduce
its carbon footprint, and purchases carbon offsets based on an annual audit to
ensure a carbon neutral footprint. For further information, or to browse our full
list of books and purchase securely, visit our website at: www.newsociety.com

Library and Archives Canada Cataloguing in Publication

Brown, Wendy, 1967–

Surviving the apocalypse in the suburbs : the thrivalist's guide to
life without oil / Wendy Brown.

Includes bibliographical references and index.

ISBN 978-0-86571-681-0

1. Sustainable living.   2. Self-reliance.   3. Suburban life.   I. Title.

    GE196.B76 2011        333.72        C2011-900039-3

**NEW SOCIETY PUBLISHERS**
www.newsociety.com

**Mixed Sources**
Product group from well-managed forests,
controlled sources and recycled wood or fiber
www.fsc.org  Cert no. SW-COC-000952
© 1996 Forest Stewardship Council

To Deus Ex Machina—

the world is a very scary place, my Dear.

You make it less so.

❧

# Contents

# Acknowledgments

I owe a great deal of thanks to so many people who either consciously or unwittingly helped me along in bringing this book to life. Our lives are intricately woven networks of people who influence us in so many, often invisible, ways. One contact leads to another and another and then, something extraordinary, like writing a book, happens, sometimes starting with something as simple as hello. Acknowledging all of those innocent contacts and conversations that ultimately led to the book you are holding would be another book in itself, but there are a few whose support during the actual writing warrant some recognition.

A very special thanks is owed to blogger "Verde" (a.k.a. Rev-Gal) who blogs at justicedesserts.blogspot.com. In 2008, she encouraged the blog world to imagine that we knew *the end of the world as we knew it* (TEOWAWKI) was imminent and that we had only twenty-one days to prepare. She challenged us to spend the next twenty-one days thinking about and blogging about the kinds of things we would do to prepare. This book is an extension of that twenty-one day blog challenge.

To Kate, who blogs at Living the Frugal Life (livingthefrugallife.blogspot.com), for coining the term "thrivalist."

To the people at New Society Publishing, without whom this project may never have been completed — Ingrid Witvoet, Editor extraordinaire, who was always available to guide me in my ignorance; Sue Custance, Ginny Miller and EJ Hurst, who added another dimension to my two-dimensional work; and Judith Brand, who patiently guided me through the editing process while I was trying to do rewrites.

To all of the wonderful people in our "village" at Centre of Movement and Fiddlehead Center for the Arts, who taught my homeschoolers while I worked on the project, and didn't scold me (much) when I was late getting my girls to class. With special thanks to: Ms. Vicky Lloyd, Sherri Fitzgerald, Andy Happel, and Caroline Rodrigue. My beautiful daughters (and I) are better for knowing you.

To Chris and Ashirah Knapp of Koviashuvik in Temple, Maine who provided a real-life example of how to take the best of the modern world and the best of the simple life and make it work. I knew what was possible, but you proved it.

To my amazing girls who have enthusiastically participated in the dramatic changes to our lifestyle, and even when we cut cable, gave away the television, turned our suburban yard into a farm, started heating with wood (which meant working all summer splitting and stacking firewood), began shopping at thrift stores, put moratorium after moratorium on our spending, and changed to a local diet, they never complained about what they didn't have. In fact, they have more fully embraced the changes than, perhaps, even their father and I have, and their appreciation for simplicity in life is a constant inspiration to me.

But most of all to Eric (affectionately known as *Deus Ex Machina*), my partner, my confidante, my spiritual advisor, my pillar, my love, my life, my in-the-flesh *god-in-the-machine*. He knows more about what I'm capable of than I do. When I think I've reached the apex, I look back and there he is with a firm hand under my rump, helping me reach that next outcrop. Without his encouragement and support, I'm not sure I would have been able to make this book a reality.

# Preface

*We have to prepare for a non-industrial future while we still have some resources with which to do it. If we marshal the resources, stockpile the materials that will be of most use, and harness the heirloom technologies that can be sustained without an industrial base, then we can stretch out the transition far into the future, giving us time to adapt.*
— Dmitry Orlov —

*Thus, the task is not so much to see what no one yet has seen, but to think what nobody yet has thought about that which **everybody** sees.*
— Schopenhauer —

Times are bad. No one will dispute that fact, now. I keep hearing talk about the need to "restore our economy," and back in 2008, back before things were as bad as they have become, I had a nice debate on my blog about "restoring the economy."

Back then, I said:

I'm not sure *we* can restore our economy, and I'm not sure....

Well, I'm not sure what that means, exactly. What part of the "economy" is it that we wish to "restore"? The part

1

where everyone owns 14 whizzi-gidgets, 13 of which don't work and none of which are even manufactured in the US? The part where the "good-paying" manufacturing jobs are outsourced overseas, because the company owners can't afford to pay Americans to make the whizzi-gidgets for the price Wal-Mart is willing to pay? Or the part where the best job in town is actually **at** Wal-Mart, and many of the whizzi-gidgets for sale there are too expensive for the employees to even purchase?

I guess my problem with this is that I'm not sure who is benefiting from the sale of the whizzi-gidget. Certainly not the retail cashier, who might make minimum wage. Probably not the truck driver who delivers it to the store. Probably not the guy who unloads it at the docks when it arrives on the container ships. Maybe not even the sailors who travel across the ocean with it. Who, then? The Chinese teenager who sits in a factory for ten hours a day fitting the plastic parts together? Sure, they all have jobs, but shouldn't there be more to life than just working so that we can afford another whizzi-gidget?

There was a time when people did meaningful work for an honest day's wages. That's the "economy" I would like to restore. I think it's wrong to pay the lowest price we can find for something, just because it's the lowest price. I think it's wrong to pay less than something is worth, because someone somewhere in the world is willing to work for next to nothing just so I can have it.

When I made my cloth feminine hygiene products, it took me close to a half hour to make each one. If I worked for the federal minimum wage, each one would cost, in labor alone, $3. For one cycle, the average woman would need at least six, and that's assuming she launders them each time she changes her pad. The initial outlay, would then be $18 — for just cutting the material and sewing all the pieces together. That doesn't even include the cost of materials, etc. Sure, they don't break, you don't throw them away, and you can use them over and over, but in our "throwaway" economy, with "disposables" costing only $6 for 24 napkins, who's going to pay $18 for just 6?

If the solution to "restore the economy" means making everything so cheap (per price and per quality) that we can just throw them away and get another one each time it's used, then I say, please don't restore the economy. Let it die, like it should, and we can be like the phoenix and raise a "new economy" out of the ashes of the old. Yes, it will be painful and messy as we crash and burn, but it's going to happen whether we accept it or not, and instead of keeping the scorched bird on life-support indefinitely while we spend precious resources fruitlessly trying to save it, we could build something different, something that is based on something real and tangible rather than on empty promises of some "better place" to be had if only we believe enough and work hard enough.

It's time to pop the fantasy bubble and see the world for what it really is. Some people wear fancy clothes, and some people don't. That's life. Our current economy has only made more clear the line between those who have the good clothes and those who buy cheap imitations (every three months) from places like Wal-Mart.

If we could use our resources more wisely (and here I mean "personal" resources, specifically, money), then, maybe, we could afford to buy one or two of the "better quality" items. But instead, I know some people whose car barely passed inspection this year, but instead of saving for

a new car (which they probably need for employment purposes as there is no mass transit system where I live), there's
a 32-inch plasma television delivery and a satellite dish in-
stallation.

Unfortunately, I don't believe these people are acting
differently than most Americans would in their situation.

What's sad is that nothing better has happened since I wrote that
post, and despite all of the warning bells and whistles and red flags
and massive pyrotechnic displays of "DANGER! DANGER!,"
most folks are still going about their daily lives as if…as if someone will push the *that was easy* button and all of this will just go…
a…way.

At this time, today, we still have time to act, rather than react-
ing when things get really bad, but we don't have much time. We
should get prepared to be without the stuff our modern lives have
made us believe are necessary to survival, and we really have to
understand the difference between what we really need to survive and what we just want. I like my Dr. Bonner's Organic Cas-
tille soap, but I won't die without it. But water? I will die without
that.

The fact is that disasters happen every day. In the last five years,
alone, hundreds of thousands of US citizens have suffered as a
result of natural disasters from hurricanes, tornadoes and flooding
to wildfires and severe winter storms. These natural disasters are
usually of very short duration but can have long-term devastating
effects. In fact, New Orleans may never fully recover to its pre-
Katrina days.

There is some good deal of wisdom, especially for those who
live in disaster-prone areas, to prepare for the inevitable. When
I was a kid and living in Alabama, not only did we practice (in
school) for tornadoes, but everyone always had on hand plenty of

flashlights and transistor radios, batteries, candles and matches. We all also knew where to go when bad weather hit, and anyone who lived in that sort of area for any length of time could tell when a tornado had touched down within a few miles just by the way the sky looked. We knew bad weather was inevitable. My guess is that most people who live on or around the Gulf and south Atlantic coastlines have some sort of hurricane preparedness kit, but I also suspect that there are a good number who do not, which is incredibly foolhardy, especially in light of Katrina's impact.

Natural disasters happen every day, and we should be prepared, but these days, with all that is happening with our global economy, a destitute housing market, a ballooning national debt, increasing unemployment and out-of-control personal debt, combined with resource depletion, there are other emergencies against which most of us should be hedging. It is very likely that the emergency we will find ourselves in will not be due to weather, but due to a total collapse of our way of life, and if (when) that happens, it will be truly devastating for this country.

The year 1929 is most often touted as the beginning of the Great Depression of the 1930s, but if one looks at the events leading up to the stock market crash in September 1929, one can gain a better understanding of the, largely avoidable, events that led up to the crash. The Great Depression was not caused by the stock market crash, but rather by easy credit. In addition, in retrospect, the Great Depression is seen as a continuous decline followed by a gradual ascent, but that is not exactly how it happened. In fact, while men in three-piece designer suits were selling apples on the street corners in Cincinnati, Ohio, people in the panhandle area of Texas and Oklahoma were experiencing a boon time, and in the early years of the Depression, many farmers in the Southwest enjoyed huge profits, which prompted them to borrow money, which resulted, as we know, in financial ruin. Further, the Great

Depression did not just abruptly end in 1939 with everyone getting back to work and having enough to eat. We entered World War II, during which the government was able to enforce things like rationing, and drafting young men into military service gave much of the youth jobs. It was not until after the war was over and our fighting men came back home that the Depression could truly be said to have ended. If we look for the end of the Depression, we would need to look into the late 40s to find it.

In short, the Depression was not an immediate global reaction to the crash of Wall Street, and the effects of the Depression were not equal across the board. Some areas of this country were truly devastated. Others continued to limp along, and still others prospered. Worldwide, some countries were completely destitute while others continued to thrive.

Given the current economic climate, the likelihood of a second worldwide depression is considerable. In fact, while some news seems to indicate that we are on a rebound, it seems more likely that this slight upswing is just that—an upswing, and at some point, the pendulum will swing back. In the summer of 2010, reported job losses were down one month, compared to the previous month, but businesses were still not hiring. New unemployment claims were down, but there were a number of factors that could skew those results to make it seem not as dire as it truly was, including the fact that a significant number of the jobless had maxed out their unemployment benefits and had neither jobs, nor the benefit of a government paycheck each week.

Despite government handouts, several large companies still filed for bankruptcy, and every day, the news media told stories of bankrupt companies and economic woes. In September 2008, it was very scary and new, especially the stock market crash that had people terrified of reliving those days of yore. That year there was a renewed interest in the 1930s Depression, and the newspapers were rife with stories by old-timers about how they had survived those times. By the summer of 2009, the sensationalism of the recession had ended, and it was just another day like all of the other days in the previous six months. Nothing new in the news, and it was all still bad. People stopped paying close attention to what was happening, and things did not seem as bad as they had seemed in 2008, but if we were really paying attention, it was worse.

By 2010, despite news stories reporting a recovery, economic collapse seemed inevitable. In fact, even some of the upbeat news stories supported the decline of the economy.

In 2006, I met a home-schooling mother from Zimbabwe, and I had the unique opportunity to witness, through sporadic email contact, the collapse of their economy. When we first met, life there was difficult, but bearable. She lived on a farm, and so they had plenty of food. But as the economic and political turmoil worsened, little necessities became harder to find. First, there were shortages of things like toothbrushes and school supplies, and she asked me to help her set up a home-school resource center for others who might wish to home-school in her country. They needed supplies like used books, pens, pencils, markers, crayons — anything. They weren't picky, as their choices were very limited there. I sent her some clothes my children had outgrown, when she told me that clothes and shoes were hard to find, and many of the charitable donations from countries like the US that were sent there ended up being sold rather than given to the needy.

Their money was all but worthless, and an average weekly grocery bill could cost in the millions of dollars. She started sending me links to websites that told of food shortages and rioting and political upheaval. Electrical service became sporadic; weeks would pass and I wouldn't hear from her. When I did, it was all bad news. They were likely to be evicted from their farm, and her husband was jailed. Her last message said she was looking to emigrate. I sent her some information about organizations she could contact in the US. I haven't heard from her in several years.

The point is that it took a long time to go from a peaceful, happy life as home-schoolers living on a productive farm in Zimbabwe to political refugees in neighboring Zambia. It did not happen overnight, or even over the span of a few weeks or months, and while historians may look back and pinpoint one significant event that seemed to be the catalyst to the whole collapse, it was actually a series of events, many of which will be overlooked by people who will later study it.

It will be, in the future, much like our knowledge of the Great Depression, which I and most of my peers learned was a result of the stock market crash of 1929. While it is true that this had a significant impact on the economic health of the United States, it is not true, entirely, that it *caused* the depression.

Other countries that have experienced economic collapse have seen similar occurrences. In his book, *Reinventing Collapse*, Dmitry Orlov talks about shortages in Russia in everything from food to general merchandise (clothing, books, toiletries) to gasoline. In his blog account of the collapse of Argentina's economy, Fernando "FerFAL" Aguirre relates similar shortages and gives advice on how to prepare, things he wishes he had had time to do, but did not. If the writing was on the wall, no one in his country saw it, but in retrospect, he can advise those of us in other parts of the world who are beginning to experience what happened there on what we can do to make our lives easier *when* it happens to us.

While I do not believe that we can prepare for every possible scenario, nor do I believe that it is possible to store everything we might possibly need forever without some way to replenish our supplies, I do believe, that like being forewarned of a natural disaster and heading to the cellar, we can mitigate the effects of an economic disaster by changing some of our habits and getting a little prepared.

Let's pretend. Let's pretend that we are like Noah, of Biblical fame, and we have been forewarned that there will be a catastrophic event in a specified period of time. We are told that we have 21 days to prepare.

Let's pretend that we know that in 21 days life as we know it will come to an end. It does not mean that *life* will cease to exist, and it does not mean that humans will be obliterated from the Earth. What it means is that all of the things we have come to expect, all of the luxuries we enjoy, all of the accoutrements of modern life that are part of our day-to-day existence will be harder to get or just no longer available. Things like on-demand grocery stores with fresh strawberries in December when there is a blizzard raging and oranges in places where oranges would never grow, an unlimited supply of gasoline, municipal water, continuous electricity, passable roads, emergency medical care (even for those with health insurance), the Internet, cable television — anything that is part of our "modern" life will be gone…in 21 days.

Twenty-one days from right now, it will happen overnight. Just like that. The light switch goes off…and does not come back on. The grocery store shelves are mostly bare, and the manager just does not know when…or if…the next supply truck will arrive. The gas station does not have lines, because there is simply no gasoline on most days, and when there is some available, it sells out before a line can even form. The tap is dry. The power grid has collapsed. Blackouts are the norm, and having electricity is an anomaly. No Internet, no cable, no cellphones.

The irony is that we really do not have to stretch our imaginations to understand much of this scenario, because all of these things have happened, recently, right here in the developed world. Hurricanes Katrina and Gustav showed what it is like when municipal water supplies are disrupted, and anecdotes from the people in Galveston relayed what it was like when delivery trucks were delayed and power outages meant that people could not access their money at ATMs. In 2008, Atlanta-area news reports showed what could happen when gasoline deliveries were stopped. The collapse of the banks in California gave us a glint of what it might look like when banks do not open their doors, but our money is tucked deep in their vaults. The Eggo shortage in 2010 and the subsequent empty freezer space showed what it would look like if our grocery shelves were not restocked. Stories from the 2008 winter storm in the Northeast, the 2009 ice storm in the Midwest and the 2010 snowstorms that devastated the mid-Atlantic states from Washington DC to Pennsylvania revealed how people coped (or failed to cope) without electricity during brutally cold weather.

For many of us, the ability to take care of ourselves without the modern conveniences we have come to take for granted is seriously lacking. The problem is that we just do not think about those kinds of things until it is too late. We do not think about what we will do in the event of a winter power outage until we wake up and the lights do not come on at the flick of a switch.

In December 2008, the Northeast was hit by a severe winter storm that knocked out power for most of us along the coastline. Everything was shut down. A couple of stores that carried things like generators and non-electric heaters opened their doors, even though they did not have power either, so that they could sell these necessary items to customers. And they sold out, within minutes. There was a waiting list, but the list was so long for generators that half the people on the list still did not have a generator when the power finally came back on four days later. Every winter there are big storms along the coast. All of the electricity that supplies our homes and businesses is delivered through wrist-thick wires that are strung between poles lining the roadways.

Think about it. The key to most modern people's health and comfort is the spark that is carried through a wire that is suspended 20 feet into the air...and just hanging there, vulnerable to wind, rain, ice, snow, downed trees and bad drivers (we have actually lost power once when a drunken driver hit a transformer).

The point is that our survival is often dependent on an incredibly unreliable and fragile system.

And we do not even acknowledge it — probably, because most of us do not think there is anything we can do.

But there is.

And the first step is to pretend that we know *the* event that changes our modern lives forever is going to happen in 21 days.

We have 21 days to prepare.

What are you going to do?

Twenty-one days.

On your mark…

Get set…Go!

# DAY 1

## Shelter

In a survival situation, for some reason, people always want to look for food first. It is like knowing that the grocery store is far away, or that there is no McDonald's around the next bend, makes people suddenly ravenous and afraid they might starve to death if they can not find some tasty bark ASAP.

I know that I can go for most of the day without eating, much. I do not *eat* breakfast (a cup of sweetened tea is breakfast). Sometimes I do not sit down and have a lunch, although I might grab a handful of nuts, a couple of crackers or some dried fruit…and a cup of tea. I drink a lot of tea.

The point is that I do not need a lot of food.

Several years ago, I was working late, because my boss was dictating a speech for a ceremony the next day, and I had been tasked with transcribing it for him, but he was not recording it. He was telling me what he wanted to say, asking me to read it back and proof it, suggest changes and fill in words when he could not think of the exact term. It was taking a very long time. I lived in a communal setting, and meals were served at designated times. There was no going to the kitchen and grabbing a tray of leftovers if I missed the meal time. If I missed getting to the dining room on time, I would miss that night's meal, and aside from having a coffee pot and a little refrigerator, I was not permitted to cook in my room.

As it got later, suddenly I was starving. Just the knowledge that I would miss a meal was enough to make me hungrier, which is crazy, because I had had lunch and breakfast. It had not even been 12 hours since my last meal.

In a lost-in-the-woods survival scenario, this is the mindset that people find themselves in, and, unfortunately, it could kill them.

> **Fact:** The average person can survive *without any food at all* for three weeks.
> **Fact:** One can die of exposure to the elements in as little as three hours.

In a true lost-in-the-woods survival scenario, all of the experts agree that the first order of business is to secure shelter.

The irony is that people, especially here in America, seem fixated on ensuring everyone has enough food, while shelter seems a secondary concern. Homelessness in some of our nation's cities is rampant (in the Los Angeles area, an estimated 70,000 people are homeless — roughly the population of Maine's largest city). The press always seems to place a greater emphasis on the food issue with regard to homelessness, but contrary to popular belief, we do not need a lot of food to survive. When faced with extreme survival, most people stumble around trying to find the tastiest bark, when in fact, they should be trying to build something in which they can escape the cold, the wet or the sun. Reality TV fans will note that the teams on the popular *Survivor* who had a comfort-able, weather-tight shelter that allowed them a good night's rest performed better and felt better than those teams whose shelter did not keep them warm or dry.

Unfortunately, here in the US, we do not look at our housing as shelter. Houses are an investment, and we talk about the places we live in terms of value and equity. These homes are not places where we plan lives, but rather one more asset in our portfolios.

When my husband and I bought our house in 1997, we be-lieved, like most Americans, that this house was temporary. We had high hopes of finding a more permanent home some unde-fined time in the future. This house was good enough for a start, but we were sure that, eventually, we would find a little place out in the country, on a few acres, where we could pursue a more self-sufficient life.

I think our dream probably sounds very familiar to most peo-ple, especially those of us who live in the suburbs and have dreams of the country life. The original American Dream had very little to do with what we modern people consider success and prosperity. It was not about having the latest and greatest gadgets, the best clothes or the right car, a big house with a picket fence and 2.5 kids. The original American Dream had to do with being self-sufficient, whether that means having a piece of land and taking care of one's own needs or owning a profitable business or having a successful career. The Dream is security, and my husband's and my vision of security was a rural home where we produce our own food.

At some point over the next eight years, it finally dawned on us that we were probably not going to move, that our dream of a rural homestead was not likely to happen, and that whatever we had hoped our lives would be would have to include what we had.

It was at that point that our house ceased to be an asset in the economic sense and started to be an asset in the survival sense. As long as we have our house, we have a place where we are safe and protected.

I lived for many years in the rural southeastern Appalachia area of Kentucky. Sixteen of the 100 poorest counties in the United States are in Kentucky, and the community where I lived was number 83. Life there could never be described as easy, and people truly did *toil*, but if you asked them, they knew they were poor, but none would have described themselves as destitute.

In fact, I recall stories about life in that area during the 1930s, when the worst thing that was happening had nothing to do with the worldwide Depression and had everything to do with trying to get corporate America to be fair. People were poor, but people in that part of the country had always been poor. Money was not something that people had, but what they did have were large gardens, land enough to raise a few animals and a house. By 20th-century suburban standards, not much of a house, but it sheltered them from rain and snow. It got cold in the winter, but there was a good coal stove (also, often used for cooking), and it got hot in the summer, but there was always a nearby creek for keeping cool.

The bottom line is that if one has shelter, everything else comes a little more easily.

The most prevalent form of housing in the United State is the single-family home, most often located in a resource desert area called "suburbia." Authors and documentarians have lambasted the suburbs as unsustainable, and *in their current incarnation*, I would not disagree. Unfortunately, one-third of the population of the United States (and a good deal of the population elsewhere) lives in what could be described as a suburb, and moving all of us out of the suburbs and into the country or into the city is not likely, especially given the short amount of time we have to react.

So, for the sake of our scenario, let's focus on what suburbanites have that is unique to their particular habitat and might, with a little imagination, be used to their advantage.

1. Suburban homes have a yard space, usually between 5,000 and 40,000 square feet (roughly, one-tenth of an acre to an acre of land). Not a lot, but more sometimes just means "more," which isn't always better.
2. Suburbs are "close" to amenities. While "close" really is subjective, and some people would say that anything within a 50-mile radius qualifies, I (and most of my survivalist fellows) would classify close as within walking or biking distance. Most adults can walk a steady, comfortable 4 miles per hour on a fairly level, fairly smooth surface, like a road or a sidewalk. Anything more than 20 miles away would probably not be "close." My suburb is 12 miles from the "city," about half that from a large "town," and only 2 miles from the town center of the seasonal resort community to which I pay property taxes.
3. Suburban homes are usually single-family residences. People who escape to the suburbs want to have some sense of privacy, but recognize that being interdependent might not be such a bad thing.
4. Suburbs do not, typically, have any businesses (except for the occasional "home business" that usually doesn't attract onsite clients, like my "virtual" office service).

In short, suburbs are residential communities where everything is carted in. We live here, but we are supported, entirely, by outside resources.

While the suburbs have been horribly maligned as "the worst misallocation of resources ever," owning a suburban home has its merits.

So, while few of us will be able to pay off the mortgage for our suburban homes within the timeline of this scenario, we should at least accept that we would be better off not moving, and that what we have is considerably better than a cardboard box.

Just for the sake of argument, however, let's consider some of the benefits of keeping our suburban homes.

First is the fact that we all have a little bit of land. True, most suburban landscapes consist of lots of inedible grass, ornamental flowers and shrubs, with an occasional shade tree to break up the monotony, but the fact is that there is land. It doesn't take much time, energy or money to build a raised bed or two and plant a few vegetables. Those authors who have seen, first-hand, the effects of collapse all say the same thing: a piece of land on which to grow food helped the people to survive the worst, and like cologne — a little goes a long way.

Second, the suburbs are close to amenities; which means that when gasoline supplies become scarce, those in the suburban areas will be close enough to urban centers to get what they need. An article about farmers in Argentina stated that there is plenty of fertile land, and farmers are growing a lot of food. Unfortunately, the people out in the rural areas are going hungry, because the food is being trucked into the urban centers. Being halfway between rural farms and urban centers, suburbanites have geography squarely in their favor, and even if we could not convince the farmers to stop in our neighborhoods, getting to the urban markets would not be as difficult as it is for those living further out.

Third, the single-family residences in most suburban neighborhoods are fairly large. The movie *Slumdog Millionaire*, about a young man who played and won the Indian version of *Who Wants to Be a Millionaire?*, featured a boy who was actually from the slums in Mumbai, India. When the filming was over, he went back to the slums. Recently, the movie production company purchased an apartment for him and his family of ten. They are currently living in luxury in a one-bedroom 250 square foot apartment. Their entire apartment would fit in one room of my house. The reality of that put things into perspective for me, and I realized that, while I've always thought my house was small (and compared to the "average" suburban house, it is), by global standards, it's a mansion.

I will go into greater detail in later chapters regarding how to grow stuff on our small suburban lots, and even how to travel from here to there in a low-energy world, but the third advantage we suburbanites have is the one that will, likely, prove the most valuable. With our big houses, we could very easily turn our suburbs into small self-sustaining, walkable communities.

One of the biggest complaints regarding the suburbs is that most of us commute to our jobs, and because we drive to these jobs, suburbanites are accused of being a drain on resources. But we don't have to drive to work. In my opinion, the worst move we made as a society was listening to Henry Ford. First, there's the whole car thing, but that aside, what Ford gave us was a system for mass production on an assembly line. He made everything more efficient and took the life right out of us. So, instead of one very well-made piece of clothing, what we have is a closet full of cheaply made shirts. Instead of one very well-made chair, we had landfills full of cheaply made and now broken pieces of furniture. We divided our lives between our homes and our work, often resulting in one or the other suffering.

That the suburbs were purposely separated from business centers is the only real design flaw in the suburban model, but there is no reason why we should accept the current standard as a fact of life, especially when it can be easily changed.

Many businesses can be adapted to a home-based setting, and in fact, most of them likely started out as a home-based business.

Like most metaphors, the term "cottage industry" likely reflects a time when manufacturing was done at home, in a cottage, if you will. Many modern entrepreneurs started out working at home. The founders of the Apple computer company began in a garage, and Mrs. Fields, reportedly, started her cookie business from her kitchen. Less than a century ago (such a small amount of time in the greater scheme of things), most business owners actually worked from home (although that wasn't the terminology used back in the day), and in older communities, this is still evident. On Main Streets across the country, storefronts are on the bottom floor of buildings with living quarters above the store. People lived where they worked.

Most suburban homes have enough space for both living quarters and "business" quarters. There's no reason not to have a living room become a dressmaker's shop, convert the utility room to a hair salon, have a cobbler's bench in a garage, or turn a basement into a brew pub.

As gasoline becomes scarcer, and the 40-mile round-trip commute becomes less possible, we will need to find new ways to make a living. Whether the exchange is with dollars or pure barter, we will still need to have something we can trade (either goods or services) to acquire what we will need that we can not provide for ourselves. Very few of us will be able to provide for 100 percent of our own needs, and it would be very useful to consider one's own talents, training, interests and education and how those can translate into a business.

Twenty-one days may be too little time to see a business become profitable, but starting to think about the possibilities, writing down some ideas, sketching out some plans and maybe even researching the codes and licensing requirements could be started and finished in that short time. The first step is to start planning ways to keep the shelter.

Because, in a survival situation, shelter is the first order of business.

What's funny, in a sad kind of ironic way, is that when I have the conversations about how we should be investing our extra money in paying off our houses or making those structures more energy efficient, I invariably end up debating why it is not a good idea to invest all of our cash in our homes, especially given how the housing market has recently buckled, and certainly, if I owed a great deal more money on my house than I could reasonably expect to pay, I might feel differently. Even with the economic downturn, however, and the housing market bubble, most houses are still worth close to what the homeowners owe, and it's worth it to keep those homes and try to pay off the debt.

So, let's suppose for a moment that my advice is heeded, and we have taken every liquid asset we have and paid off the mortgage, and then spend the next three weeks working on a business plan for a home-based business idea that we believe will support us, and then, *nothing* happens. Then what? Well, the house is paid off, which means, even if the house isn't worth as much as the original bank note, nothing is owed now. It would be kind of like paying off a car loan. Over time, the amount paid is considerably more than the car will ever be worth, but once it's paid off, it can no longer be repossessed—no matter what—and there is some security in ownership.

If things go back to the way they were before the housing bubble burst in 2008, that house, now owned free and clear, could translate into a nice little chunk of change for the owners, should they ever decide to sell.

In addition to paying off the house, we also went through the steps of writing up a business plan for a potential home-based business, in which we'd be our own boss. We've researched the laws and know what the municipal ordinances require (or prohibit) and what licenses are needed to get started. We may have even started printing flyers or doing other marketing around the community, and if we did really well, we might have even had our first customer.

In short, if *the end of the world as we know it* (TEOTWAWKI) doesn't happen…

We own our house, in the suburbs, with a nice little piece of land, far enough away from the city to be removed from all of the problems inherent to city living but close enough to reap all of the benefits. In short, if the world as we know it doesn't end, and life goes back to the way it was at the end of the 20th century, we've secured our financial future by owning a piece of fairly valuable real estate in what is a fairly desirable location, and having what could be a profitable, small business.

And that's bad, because…?

After we've committed to staying in the suburbs, we should take some steps to make sure that it is a good shelter, the first of which should be to list any repairs or upgrades that need to be done. We started painting our house two years ago, but never quite finished. We should make a point of doing that this year. There are also a few places where some of the outside trim is rotting, an invitation to insect infestations, like termites and carpenter ants, neither of which are welcome guests. Make sure the foundation is sound and the roof does not leak.

After repairs, some upgrades should be considered. The value of a properly insulated building can not be overestimated. In today's terms, insulation saves on fuel bills because of less heat/cool loss. In a lower-energy society, insulation will ensure that a warm house stays warmer when it is really cold outside, and that a cool house stays cooler when it is really hot outside. Replacement doors and windows can be incredibly expensive, but if it is in the budget, there's no better time than now to replace leaky doors and inefficient windows. While there are some low-energy techniques, like wall hangings and window quilts, that can be used to keep the temperature in our homes comfortable, the better option is to just properly insulate in the first place, and then, if heating fuel becomes scarce or we're faced with cooling our homes without AC, it will be more easily accomplished. We all know it is something we should do, and really, there is no better time than today, Day 1, to get started.

In summary, where you are, right now, is probably the best place for you to be. Make sure you can stay there, because 20 days from now, we will be a much less mobile society.

**DAY 2**

# Water

After shelter, the second most important item in a survival scenario is water.

Water.

The human body is 97 percent water. We can only live a few days without it. It helps us keep cool and stay warm; drinking lots of it helps to purge toxins from our bodies. Water is also an essential element in our homes. It keeps things clean, and in some heating systems, it keeps the house warm. It is the elixir of life, and any preparedness plan that does not account for water is doomed to fail.

For most of my life, my water has come from a municipal water supply. When I was living in the suburbs in eastern Alabama, we would occasionally have drought conditions, and our water usage would be restricted by mandate. Certain activities would be outlawed — like watering lawns and washing cars.

Generally, these days, my family limits these activities by choice, because we feel water conservation is important. I currently live in a very wet area (50% of the year, there's some form of precipitation — rain or snow); water rationing and drought have never been an issue since I moved here more than a decade ago. But we are on city water, and while it has never happened, yet (knock on wood), the potential for us to lose access to potable water is there.

The water company that supplies my water gets it from a nearby river using huge pumps to suck the water up into the treatment facility. From there, it is pumped through a network of over 200 miles of pipes that snake underground around the neighboring communities to get to my home. It costs, in 2010 figures, about $750,000 in electricity per year to deliver 8 billion gallons of water, about $1 for every 10,000 gallons. For reference, 202 gallons of water equals 1 cubic yard. We use about 54 gallons of water per day in our house, which costs about $16 per month or 50¢ per day.

Currently, 40 percent of the electricity that is used in my house is derived from hydro power, but that leaves 60 percent. Twenty-five percent of our electricity comes from natural gas. The other roughly 30 percent is from fossil fuels, coal and natural gas.

Having lived for many years in a coal mining community, I've actually had the opportunity to see a coal mine in action. All modern mining operations are heavily dependent on machinery to assist in the extraction process. Men are needed to operate the machines, but the machines are powered by fossil fuels. In addition, once the coal is pulled from the ground, it's loaded onto huge dump trucks, which transport it to the rail yards. Trains take the coal to power plants (or to ships for transportation to power plants) and then the coal is burned to produce the electricity that makes my CFL bulbs glow and powers my computer. Men fought and died to make the coal mines safer places to work and to force coal mine owners to provide a fair wage, but even the most conscientious owners can not make the mines completely safe. It's difficult, dirty and dangerous work, even with the machines, but without them, it would be worse.

The problem is that it's all related. Oil is used in the coal mines to get the coal that gives us electricity. Electricity powers the pumps that feed the water through the pipes that allow me to have this life elixir flow unheeded, on demand from my tap. If non-renewable resources are no longer available for electricity generation, the water that flows so freely out of the several taps in my house may stop.

I have thought about what we would do in that case. There is a small brook behind my house, where, in a pinch, we could get water. A mile in any direction brings me to a source of fresh water (and by "fresh" I mean "not salty") that I could carry home, filter and boil to drink. In addition, I live about two miles from the ocean, and using a distillation/desalination process, I could make the ocean water drinkable.

Both of my parents grew up on rural homesteads during the late 40s, 50s and early 60s. They remember living without electricity, central heating/cooling, television and indoor plumbing. Recently I asked my mother if she could only keep one modern convenience, which would it be, and without hesitation, she said, "Indoor plumbing."

I agree.

In the 1990s, when I was teaching in a rural community in northern Kentucky, I didn't have running water in my house for the first several weeks. I had to "borrow" buckets of water from the neighbors for washing and cooking. Carrying five-gallon buckets of water across the road is not much fun. As such, I know that depending on any one of the remote sources of water I have available to me now is not my best option. I would not have lasted the winter if I'd had to drag water across the road in a snowstorm, and walking two miles up the road to the creek.... Not the best long-term solution.

Luckily, we have several options available. Some of them are very complicated, and can be quite costly, but since we're talking about a life-preserving element, it is worth considering spending the time and money to secure.

The first (and simplest and cheapest) option is a rain barrel. In drought-prone areas, in fact, a rain barrel should be considered a necessity. We currently have two 55-gallon rain barrels that are set up to catch water as it drips (in our very wet climate, "cascades" might be a more appropriate word) off the roof. We do not have our barrels hooked up to an elaborate gutter system, because we do not have rain gutters on our roof. The reason is very complicated and has to do with the pitch (or lack thereof) of our roof

and the likelihood of ice dams forming during the winter, which creates the perfect opportunity for us to have a water catchment system "inside" the house, but ruins the insulation in the ceilings (i.e., ice dams cause water from the melting snow to pool on the flat part of our roof, and as we all know, water wants to go somewhere, usually finding its way inside the house, which is very much not a good thing).

Our rain barrels fill rather quickly and easily and are a good source of water for our gardens and our animals. We can get about eight months of use out of our rain barrels, using them every day for the gardens and the animals (we do not have to water the gardens very often, but we do have to provide fresh water for the animals, and when raising broilers during the summer, we go through a lot of water). In a pinch, we could use the water in the rain barrels (after we filtered and boiled it, of course) for drinking, cooking and bathing.

For long-term use, however, our rain barrel set-up would not be my first choice, first because we'd need to haul water into the house using buckets, which, as I already mentioned, is not the best choice. Also, in our area, the temperatures drop below freezing every night during late fall and early spring; once winter gets a good foothold, daytime temperatures stay below freezing too until the spring thaw. Frozen rain barrels do not provide water for household use.

A dug or driven well with a manual pump would be my first choice. Several neighbors have wells, but they rely on electric pumps to bring the water up from the ground and into their houses. If I were to go through the trouble of digging a well, I would want to be assured that, *no matter what*, I'd have access to my water. We lose power with enough regularity that I can not be completely confident we would have water if I depended on an electric pump.

A dug or driven well may not be the best choice for everyone, however, and rain barrels are actually illegal in some places. While this is changing, it might not change quickly enough for the survival-minded suburbanite to be prepared. An option similar to the rain barrel, but not quite so obvious, would be a cistern.

A cistern is, basically, a water holding tank. Back when cisterns were used, typically in urban areas (in fact, some of the older homes in my community — ones built at the end of the 19th century — still have cisterns in the basements, although no longer used for water storage), water would be delivered to the households. With a few modifications, an underground cistern could be used much like a rain barrel. It would just not be out in the open where it could be seen.

In a suburban setting, the cistern, instead of a rain barrel, might actually be an advantage — not the hidden part, but if land space is at a premium, which it is on the tiny suburban lot, then a water catchment system that is buried underground is certainly preferable to a large above-ground rain barrel.

Think about it, too. Buried underground, the water would be cooler in the summer and warmer in the winter than what would come out of a rain barrel. Further, in the winter, in a colder climate, rain barrels would be useless as an option for water, as the water would freeze. A cistern, buried in the ground, would not freeze.

We have a septic tank. Take a moment and forget what our septic tank has in it, but consider what our septic tank *is*. Basically, it is a watertight, concrete container with a hole in the top that is buried four feet in the ground. Using that same model, we could build an underground water catchment system. Gutters on the roof would be directed into a simple water filter made by layering sand, gravel and charcoal. The filtered water would fall into the concrete tank, which we would treat with anti-bacterial and anti-microbial agents (bleach). A hand pump would allow us to bring the clean water to the surface.

A cistern, for long-term storage, would be infinitely superior to a rain barrel, especially for people who live in areas with abundant precipitation. Here in the frozen northeast, however, we would require a really big cistern to store enough water to last us the whole winter.

The best option for those of us in a cold, wet climate is still a well.

Which reminds me, I should get to digging, and whether you're looking for water or burying your concrete tank, you should be digging, too. Nineteen days is so very little time.

# DAY 3

## Fire

Several years ago we adopted an iguana. He was named Prometheus.

He does not have anything to do with our survival preparations, except that, if one is contemplating getting a pet, and one lives in a very cold climate, I would strongly discourage any pet that needs to stay warm.

Still if one thinks about it, Prometheus was rather aptly named. In Greek mythology, Prometheus stole fire from the gods and gave it to humans so that they could stay warm. Our iguana needed to stay warm, and we used a great deal of energy (electricity in the form of a hot rock and heat lights) to make sure he did.

Our iguana knew the value of warmth, because without the proper temperatures, he would slowly die of hypothermia. He would just go to sleep, and never wake up. Humans need warmth too, and as I mentioned in the first chapter, in a survival situation, dying of exposure (i.e., freezing to death) is more likely than starving. In an extreme survival situation, the third most important element is fire. We might argue that we do not need fire to survive, but in truth, the discovery of fire, and the ability to harness it, is what gave humans the edge we needed to survive in a world where we are incredibly weak as predators and our defenses (claws, teeth, skin) are even weaker. It keeps us warm, it purifies our water, and it cooks our food.

Still, we *could* stay warm (or if not *warm*, at least not *frozen*) in our homes by bundling up.

We can make our water drinkable by filtering it and adding chemicals, but a simpler and more effective solution is boiling. Very few microbes can survive the high temperatures of boiling water, which means it is safer than just filtered water, and frankly, I am not fond of consuming chemicals.

We can eat our food raw, but some things really do need to be cooked to make them safe, and in a survival situation, we may not be able to be as particular about what we eat as we are now. In a survival situation, where food is not all that plentiful, we might be convinced to eat meat that is, maybe, not so fresh. As such, cooking it will kill harmful bacteria and/or parasites. Meat can be eaten raw, but I feel more comfortable with a little charbroiling, and I can not praise the flavor of smoked meat highly enough. Other foods have to be cooked to be digestible, including some important staples like rice, beans, potatoes and wheat.

Having fire ensures our continued health and well-being. The ideal for those of us who live in the suburbs is to have a safe place for a fire inside our homes. Fire in the house gives us heat and a way to cook food and heat water. My option is a wood stove. A properly sized wood stove can heat an entire house, regardless of where it is located. Ours is on the outside west-facing wall. The bedrooms are as far from the wood stove as they can be, but the stove manages to keep the rooms habitable, if not tropical, even on the coldest of cold days. The advantage to having the chimney on an outside wall is that we can burn just about any wood, and there's less chance of a chimney fire destroying our house. We like to burn pine, because it dries fast and burns hot. Many people will not burn pine in a fireplace or wood stove because they are concerned about chimney fires from creosote build-up, but because our chimney is on an outside wall, there is less chance of buildup. Because many people do not like burning pine, we end up with a lot of free wood from trees that have been damaged during spring storms.

The bonus to having a wood stove as our primary heat source is that we can use the top of our wood stove as a cook surface and have prepared many pots of hot soup, cooked a great number of fried delights and even baked bread using an inverted kettle over the bread pan to capture the heat.

Most of the homes I have lived in had a fireplace or a wood stove. While fireplaces provide a nice backdrop for a romantic evening, they are horribly inefficient for anything other than adding ambience to a room. They do not provide much heat, as most of it goes up the chimney with the smoke. In addition, if the chimney is not properly constructed, a fireplace will allow too much smoke into the room, and if the flue is not closed when the fireplace is not being used, some chimneys actually allow cold air into the house.

There are many suggestions for making fireplaces a more efficient heat source, but when all of the information is boiled down, what's left is the fact that a fireplace is just a very poor option. None of the efficiency suggestions are completely safe or effective, but some heat is better than none. I would never install a fireplace, but if my house already had a fireplace, I would install a fireplace insert, which is, essentially, a wood stove set inside an existing fireplace and using the existing chimney. Inserts come in many different designs; several offer a cook top surface, so that the insert works like a free-standing wood stove.

An open fireplace is also very poor for cooking. Certainly, it can be done with some creativity and the proper tools. Suspending food over the fire using a skewer or spit (for cooking meat and vegetables rotisserie-style) is a fast and easy way to cook on a fireplace. Foil-wrapped items can be placed near or even in the fire for a baked meal. For the longer term, however, an investment in some cookware is imperative.

The cast-iron Dutch oven or a camp oven was made for cooking on an open fire and works well in a fireplace. These little beauties can be placed right in the fire to make everything from stew to cornbread. In fact, we have used our camp stove in our outside firepit, and everything cooked fairly quickly—even in the pouring rain. Dutch ovens are also useful in a modern-day kitchen to reduce energy usage. A camp stove is a natural in "retained heat" cooking techniques (when the food is taken off the heat source and covered or insulated in the pan so that it continues to cook, even as it slowly cools). For more information about this technique, research the Haybox Cooker.

In a worst-case scenario, a fireplace is better than nothing, which, unfortunately, is what a lot of suburbanites have—nothing.

Not to despair, however, because there is a very simple solution. While it would better to have the fire inside, one can always build a very simple firepit outside for cooking, and even use the fire outside to provide some heat inside—without burning down the house. Because I live in a cold climate (but was, mostly, raised in a warm one), heat is a real concern for me, and so I started looking into lower-energy alternatives for home heating, especially for people who were not fortunate to have a woodstove. The answer came from the most unexpected place. One winter, my family and I participated in an outdoor skills class, and we learned to build shelters in which we could survive a freezing night using only our own bodies as heat. The key was a very small, well-insulated space.

Using that same principle, we suburbanites can have heat in our homes from the fires we build outside. What's funny is that we already know how to heat our spaces, if we really think about it. The simplest way to get the fire inside without having a fire inside is to put something that will retain heat inside the fire, like a rock and then bring that thing inside.

Using the idea of a small space (like our debris shelters that are heated with just our bodies) and heated rocks, suburbanites could provide enough heat to be comfortable inside an unheated home. The first step is to close off one room, preferably a room with few outside walls or windows. The next step is to heat large (big enough so that they slowly lose heat, but small enough that they can be safely transported from the fire to the house) *non-porous* rocks in the fire outside, and then bring them inside the house and put them into a fireproof container so that they can radiate heat into the room. Think *sauna* without the steam. At the end of the day, when the rocks have cooled a little, but are still warm, they can be wrapped in a towel and taken to bed to warm the sheets.

After I started looking for small-space heating options, I found some information about the Japanese *tatsoi*, which is a low table over which a thick blanket has been laid, the ends of draping to the floor. In the evening, the family gathers around the *tatsoi* with their feet under the blanket. They take meals and play games and generally gather together for the evening. Because the table surface is warm, it has the added benefit of serving as a warmer for the food. Using a combination of rocks warmed in the fire outside and a *tatsoi*, we could have a very comfortable place to have meals and commune with family members in the evening — even without any indoor heat source at all. In fact, many Japanese homes have neither insulation nor heat.

Firepits are a very simple solution, but if we are to depend on a fire outside for cooking and heating, we will probably want something a little more permanent. Back in the 1970s, a source of amusement for the non-suburbanite was the barbecue pit that so many suburban homes seemed to include. Some of them were incredibly elaborate affairs complete with an outdoor fireplace, a padded seating area, plumbing and paved floors. Recreating these havens, perhaps a little more utilitarian and not quite so showy, would be incredibly beneficial, especially to people who live in warmer climates, where an outdoor kitchen is preferable to a fire in the house.

We are working on building an outdoor kitchen. The design will include a rocket stove and a masonry oven, and as we plan to use it when we boil sap in the spring, a covered area would be ideal. We would also use the area for canning in the fall. In between, we plan to cook out there, especially bread in our masonry oven, and use it as an outdoor living space.

Whether you use a simple pit or build an outdoor kitchen, once you have a place for the fire, you will need to be able to light it. Certainly, matches are the preferred method, but what if the unthinkable happens, and matches just are not available? Making matches is certainly a possibility. Salt peter, which is a key element in match-making, can be made by filtering urine through wood ash. The crystals that form are salt peter, and these crystals could be used in match-making.

Of course, chemistry has never been my forte, and like most Americans, I am still a little squeamish about using my bodily fluids (I am still struggling with trying to convince myself to pee in a bucket so that I can save the nitrogen-rich fluid for my garden). So, instead of learning to make matches, I have purchased a handy little tool called a magnesium fire starter, which is used by scraping off a quarter-sized pile of magnesium into a small pile of tinder and then striking the flint surface with a knife to create a spark, which catches the magnesium and then the tinder. My husband has even gone further and has learned to start a fire using a bow drill.

Of course, wood as fuel is not available in all parts of the country. In places where whole forests were razed to make the suburbs, it is likely that the only trees are the juvenile ones planted during the "landscaping" phase of the build-out, and if there is only one tree per household, it should probably be left in the ground. I will, however, talk about some tree options later that can be planted to provide both food and fuel without the need to take down the whole tree.

So, what do we do if we do not have the option of wood for cooking and heating?

Methane gas is one alternative for a renewable fuel. Americans do not know a lot about it, because we have never needed to use it, since other forms of energy are so cheap and plentiful. What most of us do not realize, however, is that after constructing a methane digester, making the gas can be virtually free.

A typical digester consists of a slurry tank, a bleed valve and an outlet for the gas. Slurry is a mixture of water and some biomatter, the most popular being animal manure. The digester works by combining the manure and water in the slurry tank. The manure should be fresh, and any large chunks should be broken down so that the anaerobic action inside the tank is faster. Once the gas has been bled out of the tank, what is left can be used as fertilizer for the garden. It is a perfect closed system, and on a large farm, methane digesters can provide gas not only for cooking and heating, but also for the production of electricity.

Unfortunately, we in the suburbs do not have so much manure. We do, however, have kitchen wastes, and a company in India has been experimenting with methane digesters that use vegetable leavings to fuel the digester. The end product in the food waste digesters is water, which can be used to water the garden. These are not currently available in the United States, unfortunately.

Two of the companies that have pioneered the technology in India are experimenting with methane digesters that use "huma-nure" to create the necessary anaerobic activity, and there is some thought that a typical suburban septic tank might be converted to take advantage of the methane production during the breakdown of the solids.

We do not have to wait until we have a fancier option. There are dozens of plans for simple digesters — enough for some cooking fuel, or, potentially, enough methane to operate a small gas heater — on the Internet on websites like YouTube. Finding plans for a simple digester should be step one, and finding fuel for it should be step two.

Looking back to mythology, however, we can find one more option for our heating and cooking needs in the story of Icarus, who discovered the power of the sun's energy. Solar cooking and solar passive heating are options that should be considered. In fact, like the methane digesters, the Internet is rife with plans for DIY solar window heaters.

In a lower-energy society, finding a source of fuel that can be used for heating and cooking that is not dependent on fossil fuels will be imperative. The important thing to remember is that one size does not fit all, and that there is no absolute solution that will work in every situation. In many places, it will be wood, or charcoal (a wood derivative). In other places, the sun will heat our homes and cook our food. Still other places will find that methane production is the best option, and it is very likely that something else, entirely, will be what some people choose. With only 18 more days to go, finding a way to harness the power of fire should happen sooner rather than later.

DAY 4

# Cooking

It is logical to follow a discussion of fuel options with a discussion of cooking techniques. In a lower-energy world, the fuel of choice, for most of us, will be wood, but it is not readily available everywhere, and frankly, making wood the primary fuel is not much better than totally depending on oil. Using too much of a good thing, as we are now learning, leads to depletion, and deforestation has devastated large portions of our world, resulting in disastrous erosion problems and desertification, and loss of habitat leading to the extinction of many species. As Dr. Seuss pointed out in his tale *The Lorax*, cutting down all of the trees is not a good thing.

Luckily, as with most things, we have options. One low-fuel option for cooking is a rocket stove; it uses wood but in very small amounts, and the amount of heat energy it produces far surpasses the amount of fuel it requires. It is well worth building one.

The basic design involves an insulated tube with an opening at the bottom where the fire is built and an opening at the top where the heat and smoke escape. The simplest stoves are built using two cans nested one inside the other. More complex models are built using masonry. Mine will be a permanent fixture in my outdoor kitchen. We will use it during sugaring season, canning season and probably all summer long, when it is too hot for the wood stove to be lit inside.

A rocket stove, because of the tiny amount of fuel it requires, is appropriate for just about any location, but it has its limits. I can boil water on the rocket stove or fry up a mess of eggs, but baking a loaf of bread would be a bit more of a challenge.

For baking, my solution is a masonry oven, my low energy "range," which will be built next to the rocket stove. This oven can be a very simple design that includes a fire chamber and a chimney. It needs to be fairly well sealed, and it needs a door for the fire chamber. Basically, a fire is built inside the chamber. Once the chamber gets hot, the fire is scraped out and the bread is put right inside the hot stove. The bricks hold the heat for a good long time, and I hear that bread baked in a wood-fired oven is some of the best in the world. Other things can be made in the oven, as well, although it is not recommended for meat dishes.

The cob oven is a popular style of masonry oven that uses clay-infused straw to build a honeycomb-shaped structure. A simpler oven can be made using cinder block and fire bricks.

Plans for both a rocket stove and a masonry oven (including the cob oven) can be found on the Internet, and there are also a lot of very good books on the subject. Since time is of the essence, investing in a book with plans for several designs would be a good option. Both the simplest rocket stove and a masonry oven can be built for free or very cheaply with recycled, found or foraged materials.

While wood cooking is probably the best option for the cold northeast with its average of six hours of sunlight per day, all year, there are places with plenty of sunshine, and not so much wood. As such, solar cooking is probably the best option for these places.

A basic solar oven uses trapped heat to cook, and the simplest solar oven is made using a flat box, like a pizza box, with foil attached to the inside and flap of the box and a clear plastic wrap across the top opening. Larger models can be made using slightly larger boxes. A very simple and almost free solar oven can be built using nested cardboard boxes with plastic wrap, Plexiglas or recycled windows. As with the masonry stoves, there are plans on the Internet, and there are also several very good books. *Sun Cooking* has some great plans for both a cardboard solar oven and a solar burner, for things like soups and heating water. Of course, there are those of us whose mechanical skill stops at flipping a light switch. For us, there are several manufactured solar ovens available, including hybrid electric models.

Regardless of the oven, though, the concept is the same. Food is placed in a dark, heat-trapping container, under a clear, usually glass, door. Light from the sun is then reflected into the oven, and the food cooks.

Another cooking option is to build a simple methane digester, which I mentioned in the previous chapter as a heat option. Animal manure is the most popular biomass, but one can also use kitchen wastes or other organic materials. There only needs to be some organic material for the bacteria to eat inside an airtight container, and the end result will be methane gas. A very simple digester can be built using a five-gallon water bottle, like those used in a water cooler, but there are many designs on the Internet for methane digesters, from the really small water bottles to permanent concrete chambers buried in the ground.

Perhaps the simplest cooking option is a candle; although what one can cook using this method is limited to, basically, things that can be heated, like water or soup. A candle placed under an inverted tin can makes what is known as a "hobo stove." We used a variation of this when I was a Girl Scout, a stove consisting of a large, inverted can (usually a coffee can) with a small opening at the bottom. We took a second small can (usually a tuna fish-sized can) and made a Sterno burner out of it using cardboard that was curled into the can and then covered with melted wax. The cardboard would burn very slowly, and the flame was controlled by using the lid of the tuna can as a damper. The tuna can was slid through the opening at the bottom of the inverted coffee can, and cooking was done on top. I had the best ever scrambled eggs, bacon and pancakes cooked on our homemade camp stove.

For long-term cooking options, wood, solar or methane gas would be the best choices, but the camp stove and the hobo stove are fun things to have, just because, and they're cheap to make and maintain.

The bottom line is that we need to eat to survive, and gnawing a raw potato will not be pleasant. We must have a way to cook our food. Without electricity or natural gas, we will need other options, and all three that I have mentioned could be easily used in a suburban setting in the long term. Acquiring the necessary supplies now, though, is important, as materials like large cans (such as ones that hold coffee) might not be as readily available in a lower-energy world.

Seventeen days to go. How will you cook your food?

# DAY 5

# Food— Stocking Up

I hang out online at a lot of places where the sense of doom is strong. It bothers me, though, when I read about the kinds of plans people are making in preparation for an uncertain future. A lot of emphasis is being placed on stocking up on items like bottled water and canned food, and in the news are stories of doomers who are buying Meals Ready to Eat (MREs) by the case and hiding them in cellars or underground bunkers. My concern is that they are being really short-sighted. For some emergency situations, it might be prudent to have 45 cases of MREs, but for most people, especially those of us preparing for a potential, life-changing event, there is no such thing as a life-time supply of *Meals Ready to Eat.*

At some point, all prepackaged food reaches its expiration date. If I am starving, I know I will be more concerned with getting food (any food) into my body than I will about the consequences of eating expired food, but having been in the military and having depended on MREs for part of my sustenance, I would rather not just eat because I am hungry. I know, from experience, that almost any fresh food, even seriously greasy bacon and blue eggs, is better than eating MREs more than once in a 24-hour period. If I have to depend on prepackaged food that I have purchased in bulk and stored in my basement, it is unlikely that my choice will be MREs, but rather something I can use to make some tastier meals than the food packaged in those plastic sleeves.

Of course, that is an extreme example. Most of the recommendations are for storing some basic supplies, like 400 pounds of wheat berries (and grinding equipment), which is not a horrible idea. Wheat berries are fairly versatile, and can be ground into flour, boiled to make a hot cereal, like oatmeal, or sprouted for a special green treat during the winter. Sprouts can even be used to make a special bread used in a raw foods diet (research Ezekiel bread for more information). The problem with this kind of plan is future availability. If one's food storage is supported by wheat as the primary staple, and one eats all of one's wheat, or worse, the lid is not securely fastened and water gets into the store of wheat turning it rancid…or a mouse gets into the berries and…. If wheat is the primary staple, and something happens to the wheat, but the grocery stores are no longer open, because the transportation network that supplied them collapsed, and Wal-Mart closed its doors for good six months ago, and the Internet has been down for a year so there is no online ordering, and the feed store does not stock wheat, how will the ruined or depleted stores of wheat be restocked?

If wheat is not grown in large enough quantities to feed the entire population where one lives, wheat should not be a staple in the food storage preparations.

No non-native stockpiled food should be a staple, because at

some point those items may become either too expensive to purchase or just unavailable. A better idea is to stock up, in season,
on locally grown food, and other items, stock up, but only for occasional use.

Some people will suggest storing enough food for a specified
period of time, which is a good idea. I live in the northeast, and
during part of the year, food does not grow. For people like me
who eat a local diet, stocking up is part of life. I grow what I can,
buy the rest from local farmers and do a lot of canning, freezing
and drying of food during the growing season. For meat, during
the summer, we raise chickens and rabbits, which we butcher and
store in the freezer. We also purchase meat to freeze in large quantities (pork and beef) from local farmers. Fortunately, at the moment, we have several local dairy farms nearby, and so we have a
year-round supply of milk for cheese, yogurt and butter.

Over the years, we have been transitioning our diet away from
those things we can not find in our local food shed, because I have
some very strong concerns about food fatigue. If we have become
accustomed to eating yeast bread at every meal, and we find that
flour is suddenly no longer available, it could be a problem, especially for children whose favorite food is peanut butter and jelly
(and encouraging peanut butter as a favorite food in a place where
peanuts do not grow is not wise either).

After a few years of exploring our local food shed, we have
managed to make some big changes in our diet. Our main staple
food, especially during the winter, is potatoes. We eat potatoes
several times per week. I like potatoes because they are easy to prepare and are incredibly versatile. Our favorite is oven roasted with
onions in olive oil, but we also like them boiled, hashed, baked and
mashed. They can be paired with meat as a side dish or roasted
with other root veggies and some chicken sausage and served as an
entrée. With a tiny portion of meat, some broth and half a dozen

potatoes, we have a hearty and filling stew. Served with or without homemade bread, it is enough to fill our bellies and is especially welcome on a cold winter's eve.

Apples are another of our long-storage foods. Both potatoes and apples grow prolifically in our colder climate and are available from a number of different sources. Apples are almost as versatile as potatoes. We eat them raw, in season, when they're fresh and crisp, but once they start to get mealy in mid-December, we usually cook them. Baked apple crisp is probably my children's favorite way of eating apples, other than applesauce, which is an awesome accompaniment to any meal with crisp potatoes and spicy meat. A regular winter meal consists of applesauce, seasoned pork chops and roasted potatoes.

We like to pair our apples with cranberries to make cran-apple sauce, a tangy sweet treat served like applesauce. We've also cooked apples with pumpkin puree. Applesauce bread is delicious, as are apple cake and apple muffins, and applesauce can be used as a substitute for oil in baking things like cakes. Dehydrated apples are better than candy. Our children love apple cider, and the adults love (home-brewed) hard apple cider, both of which we usually have in quantity.

At the moment, we still buy flour, sugar, coffee, tea, rice, oatmeal and olive oil in bulk quantities, because at the moment, they are readily available at the local grocery store. We are still working on making the transition and finding alternatives to these. We have these certain items that we buy large quantities of, but they are not primary foods and are used as a supplement to the things we buy locally.

We have some favorite spices, like cinnamon, cumin, nutmeg and cloves, which we use fairly regularly (especially cumin, my favorite in meat dishes). Most of the herbs we use are home-grown and dehydrated (including thyme, oregano, basil, sage, tarragon, chives, garlic, onions, marjoram, lavender, rosemary, lemon balm and peppermint).

And while I enjoy cinnamon in my applesauce, which is best sweetened with a bit of sugar, I know that we will need to find alternatives, and long-term, being dependent on any of the items, even for a portion of our diet, will be dangerous. That is not to say that we can not have those items as a treat. It is unlikely that flour, salt, coffee, tea and sugar will completely disappear, given that all of them have been widely traded for hundreds of years, but when my stores of those items are depleted, the question is, will I be able to afford to buy them? And if the choice is between having sugar for my tea, or having tea at all, and having a good pair of shoes, I am thinking the answer to the question of whether I can afford it may be no. If those items are a staple in my family's diet, not having them will be an issue, but if they are an occasional treat, we would enjoy them while we had them, but not enough to go bare-footed in the winter. We would be satisfied with the other things we had without any intense cravings.

So, what are some alternatives to storing non-local food items? Here in Maine, instead of wheat flour, buckwheat is available. We will not have any yeast bread, but we would still have some great pancakes.

Another widely overlooked option is acorns, which are incredibly versatile. We also have acorns in larger quantities than most of us could ever use. They are everywhere, and most people consider them a nuisance. Properly prepared, acorn flour is a potential alternative to wheat flour. Although it is probably not going to make a great loaf of bread, acorn flour cookies are delicious. Acorns can also be roasted and ground and used as an alternative to coffee, although the flavor isn't as rich or as satisfying as coffee, and an acorn beverage lacks that caffeine kick coffee drinkers crave.

It's not fun to contemplate having to give up things we enjoy, but what I've discovered in my (not terribly) long life is that it's much easier to give up a thing by choice than by force, and if I can break my addiction to tea now, when I have the choice, and I still have the strength and ability to find alternatives, so much the better. What most Americans call "tea" is made from the prepared leaves of the *camellia sinesis* shrub, which grows in places like India, Japan, China and North Carolina. There is, in fact, a nursery here in the United States that grows and sells the *camellia sinesis* shrub for about $30 each. Unfortunately, like many very desirable food plants, it can not survive a Maine winter, and so for those of us living up here, tea may become one of those special treats rather than our current everyday beverage. As a daily tea drinker, I could not be more disappointed. I really (*really*) like my ten daily cups of tea, and finding an alternative is very difficult.

There is no substitute for real tea, just as there is no substitute for real coffee, but an alternative to *camellia sinesis* green tea could include any combination of great herbs that do grow in Maine. Pine tree tea has a similarly satisfying bite and provides a slew of immune-boosting vitamins. It is especially soothing and useful as a tea to combat the cold and flu. Sage is another herb that makes a lovely tea, and paired with lemon balm has a nice citrusy flavor. The best thing about tea, whether herbal or the traditional *camellia sinesis*, is that there really is no better beverage, either hot or cold, but if *camellia sinesis* doesn't grow where you live, it is probably a good idea to wean off it, because caffeine withdrawals are not pretty, even in the best of times.

Sugar is something else that I enjoy too much, and for which I will need to find an alternative. We already tap our maple trees, and we have maple syrup, which is not terribly difficult to make. The hardest, most time-consuming part is boiling the sap to make syrup. At a 40:1 ratio (40 gallons of sap yields 1 gallon of syrup), that is a lot of boiling, but it is worth it, as there is no substitute for real maple syrup. Maple sugar is just as sweet and lovely as cane sugar, and there is no equal to maple candy made by pouring hot syrup on clean snow.

Honey is another alternative to sugar and can be used in any recipe where a maple flavor may not be desired. Much healthier than sugar, honey is actually good for treating a number of different ailments, including cold symptoms, and has been shown to be effective in smoking cessation programs. Honey is a perfect and complete food, and has a storage life of…forever. It does not spoil. Honey is produced all over the United States, and as wonderful as the honey is, the bees are that much more beneficial. I will talk more about bees as livestock later.

Rice is another of those recommended storage foods that simply does not grow in most areas of the United States. White rice can be stored for a very long time, but has little nutritional value, making it a poor choice as a dietary staple to begin with. Many people value rice as a protein source, but it is incomplete without beans (which will grow just about anywhere and should be part of one's food stores). Brown rice goes rancid in a matter of months, and so, in a worst-case scenario, the best we could hope for would be a six-month supply of rice, and then, none. It does not make sense to waste money for a food item that will only be available for a maximum of six months with the potential of not being replenished. While a lot of people may argue with this point, the fact is that rice crop yields were significantly affected by extreme weather patterns in 2007 and 2008 resulting in several rice-producing countries refusing to export their crop. The idea that rice may no longer be available in areas where it does not grow is not terribly far-fetched.

Oats do grow in Maine, but take up a lot of crop land, which may be better used to grow the more calorie-dense potatoes, or would more likely be used as animal fodder than human food. Depending on oats as a dietary staple may be as dangerous as depending on rice or wheat.

This leaves us in the northeast with very few grain alternatives, except corn, which is a grain, a grass, actually, and which does grow in Maine. Field corn, which is very different from the popular sweet corn, has a long shelf life when dried. Most of us would recognize field corn as corn meal or popcorn (which can be ground into corn meal). When the first settlers to the Maine coast and the Massachusetts colonies arrived, they were given the gift of corn by the natives, who grew corn, beans and squash together in a configuration dubbed the "Three Sisters." A diet based on those three crops would work just about anywhere, and because these are grown together, the area needed to grow them is much smaller. In small spaces, like our suburban lots, any plants that can be grown densely, and companionably will always be a good idea.

I do not (entirely) disagree with stockpiling food. In fact, for those living in climates like Maine's, where we have a very short growing season, food preservation and storage should be an integral part of our lives. When it comes to talking about preparedness, what concerns me most is hearing the recommendations for storing foods that are common in our industrialized food chain, i.e., widely available at the grocery store, but that are not common in places where local foods are sold, like the farmer's market. I have never bought flour, sugar, tea, coffee, rice or oats in any quantities, large or small, from a local farmer (although I have found Maine-grown oats and flour at the health food store, and there is a company near the Canadian border that grows buckwheat, which they sell in the grocery store).

Certain foods that have been available for hundreds of years through trade routes may still be available…but they may not, and the best course of action would be to eliminate those items from our diets, except as treats. I would hate to never taste chocolate again in my life, and I think it would be a shame if my grandchildren never know the taste, but hinging my entire diet on something that is not available where I live is foolhardy, and I cannot say it in enough ways.

If we have it stockpiled and it is something we eat every day, and we run out, but cannot replenish, we will be hungry. As a mother, I am particularly concerned about food fatigue in my children. I have three lovely girls who are kind and gentle and easy-going in almost every way, except when it comes to the food they eat. I always swore I would not have food battles with my children, but I have, because one of my girls is the pickiest eater alive, and getting her to eat anything that's not wheat-based is a struggle (although she does like strawberries and apples). We have been slowly transitioning to a diet that consists mostly of foods that are available where we live, and I have noted that my daughter will often turn up her nose at the local food, but when we indulge ourselves and buy the non-local items, which are more familiar, she will all but binge. Because I am aware that this could be a serious problem when non-local, wheat-based foods are no longer available in the northeast (or are only minimally available), I am very concerned about what she will eat when the time comes.

Most of us have never had to worry about food fatigue or appetite fatigue. With our on-demand grocery store system, the problem is too many choices, not too few, and so the idea that a person could starve to death when there is food to eat is just ridiculous. But it happens, usually in the very old or very young. When one goes from having every craving immediately satisfied to eating rice and beans, 3 meals per day, 7 days a week, 30 days a month, 365 days a year, one may stop eating altogether. And when it comes to my incredibly picky eater, that's my biggest fear—that she will stop eating, because dinner is sautéed wild greens and quiche. So,

I have spent the past two years changing our diet to include mostly local foods and to eliminate, as much as possible, our dependence on grains as a staple.

Most of the United States is rich in fertile soil (even the sterile suburbs) where thousands of plants grow wild. There are more edible plants than there are poisonous plants, and statistically, we have a better chance of eating something that will do no harm than we do of eating something that will kill us. As such, there is just no reason for anyone to starve to death in the United States. The problem is not that we don't have enough to eat, or that our food will run out when the industrial food machine grinds to a halt, but rather that we do not know how to eat what's there and free for the taking.

There are only 16 more days to go. It is time we started learning how to eat in our local food shed, and the first stop should be the farmer's market, because what the small, local farmers are growing will likely be what we can count on having to eat when the trucks are no longer delivering Chef Boyardee's trademarked Beef-A-Roni in a can.

# DAY 6

## Food— Long-Term Storage

I did not grow up learning how to preserve food. From the day I was born until I was in my teens, I lived in apartments or in the suburbs, and food, for me and most of my neighbors, came from the grocery store. My first experience with gardening and canning came — at roughly the same time — when I was 15. The previous year, my father had retired from a career in the military, and we moved to his rural hometown and lived in a rented house in a former coal camp community.

My grandmother always had a huge garden, most of which she would harvest and preserve for the winter. She had jars upon jars of home-canned food in her cellar, and when we visited during the summer, I can remember stringing green beans on thread to dry for storage. When I was little, we were never permitted to help with the canning, or perhaps it was that most of the canning took place in the late summer and early fall, when we had returned home to await the new school year. As such, it was not until I was a young teenager, far more interested in other activities, that I was given my first opportunity to learn the joys of food storage techniques.

I remember canning tomatoes being a long, difficult and smelly job, and I didn't enjoy it. Neither was I much help, and I imagine that after only a few minutes of listening to my less than enthusiastic prattle, my mother and grandmother told me that I had helped enough.

Thus, it was not until almost two decades later, after I had traveled the world and had a few kids, and finally settled down to grow some roots that I was given the opportunity to, once again, try my hand at canning. My first home-canned food was applesauce, which I made with my mother-in-law after my husband and I had picked something like 60 pounds of apples during my first-ever visit to a pick-your-own orchard. My husband and I were probably a little overzealous with our picking, but it being our first time,

we did not know how to gauge when we had enough, and three bushel bags of apples later (it seemed like a reasonable number before we started picking), we had to figure out, quick, what to do with all of those apples, and so with the help of my mother-in-law, I made applesauce.

My annual canning season has expanded to include all sorts of things I never thought I would put into a jar, and not only do I feel that I have mastered the boiling water canner, but I am also comfortable (mostly) with the pressure canner.

What I learned in the beginning was that canning does not take any particular skill, and neither does it take any special equipment. For the first decade after I started canning, my supplies included jars with rings and lids, a large stainless steel pot, some run-of-the-mill kitchen tongs, a wide-mouthed funnel and . . . well, that's it. I did not have any fancy canner or those specially designed canning tongs for lifting jars out of the boiling water. Neither did I have a special boiling water canner, although I used to look at them longingly in catalogs — what with their lovely speckled blue design, and those nifty lifting racks. I thought, if I could just have one of those. . . . Eventually, I learned that I did not really need one of those. My big pot holds seven quart jars, and with having only the most rudimentary supplies, I still manage to store an incredible amount of food.

From stories my mother tells me, my grandmother didn't have any fancy equipment, either. Before she had her electric stove, my grandmother would have one of her boys dig a shallow pit outside in which they would build a fire. Then my grandmother would put a big washtub over the fire, add the jars of whatever was to be canned and cover them with water. That was her equipment — a washtub (that probably served double-duty many times over for bathing and laundry), and she managed to preserve enough food for her family of 13 to survive an inhospitable winter deep in the

Appalachian mountains of southeastern Kentucky, where grocery stores often weren't an option, and even if they had been, they didn't have a car, and my grandmother never learned how to drive.

Having asserted that no particular equipment is needed to can, I am now going to completely contradict myself and state that pressure canning requires a special pan that includes a pressure gauge/steam outlet on top. My grandmother canned her green beans in a simple water bath, but that's something I would never do, because the low acidity of green beans makes this not a very safe option. Green beans can be canned at home but should be processed in a pressure canner, which can be purchased in most stores that sell canning supplies and housewares.

There are two types of pressurized cooking pots. One is a pressure cooker, which allows food to be cooked quickly, using less energy, and the other is a pressure canner, which can be used to speed-cook food, but can also be used for preserving food in jars. Typically, a pressure canner is bigger than a pressure cooker so that it can accommodate quart-sized jars. They are often used interchangeably, but in the interest of safety, a pressure canner should be used in food preservation and not a pressure cooker. The difference is in the ability to adjust and monitor the pressure inside the pan. With a pressure cooker, the pressure can not be adjusted as it can with the pressure canner. Many foods require a different pressure setting in order to ensure that they are safe to store at room temperature. The pressure canner will have a temperature gauge, a little weight (or "jiggly") on top, and a steam outlet. A pressure cooker will usually have only the steam outlet with a "jiggly."

There are dozens of resources specific to canning food, and care does need to be taken. I will not offer any specific information about which foods need to be pressure canned and which only need a boiling water bath, because people who know a lot more than I do have already written the book. I will mention that just about any fruit can be made into a sauce (like applesauce or strawberry/rhubarb sauce) or preserves/jelly (with or without pectin), and they only need a boiling water bath. Most vegetables will need to be pressure canned. The difference is due to the acidity of the food, and foods that are more acidic do not require the higher temperatures during the canning process that pressure canning provides.

Of course, I am sure there are people out there who are thinking, "So, help me. Where do I start?" And my suggestion is to start with apples and strawberries. They are almost foolproof, and as long as the jar seals, the contents are safe.

Another way to preserve food is through drying, one of the two ways that Native American tribes preserved their food. Many food items can be dried, and we have probably done most of them. Most people have had some sort of dried food before and probably did not even realize it. When I was growing up, we ate a lot of cup-a-soup and similar dried soup mixes, all of which contain dehydrated foods to which we added boiling water to "cook." Some better known dried foods are raisins, which are dried grapes and jerky, which is dried meat.

Several years ago, before my husband and I started worrying about preserving a harvest, indeed, before we even had a garden to harvest, we bought a dehydrator, a nifty little machine that uses electricity to circulate warmed air up through several trays. The warm air sucks the water out of the food. The dehydrating process allows food to be stored in an airtight container at room temperature, because without water, bacterial growth (what causes food to go bad) is inhibited. Using an electric dehydrator is not the only way to dry food, however. We also dry herbs by hanging them in a dry place with good air circulation out of direct sunlight, like in a hallway.

Another way to dehydrate food is to use a solar dehydrator, which works like our electric dehydrator but uses the sun as the heat source and natural convection rather than a heating element with a fan. There are several plans for solar dehydrators, the most basic of which is a mesh bag that can be suspended from a tree branch but works best in a very dry region (decidedly *not* Maine). More complicated designs use radiant heat that is funneled into an insulated box where the food is set on trays. Of course the most creative solar dehydrator I have heard of, but never used, is the inside of a parked car with the windows all rolled up. The point is that there are a lot of options for designs. If neither a solar dryer nor an electric dryer is available, one can use a regular oven set at a very low temperature (not more than 200°F). The key to dehydrating is to be sure that the food is cut into very thin strips and placed in a single layer on a surface that allows warm air to circulate around the entire surface of the food.

Many foods can be dehydrated, from meats to vegetables. In fact, we bought our dehydrator all of those years ago because we wanted to make our own jerky, which is incredibly expensive to buy but pennies to make. More recently, I've included all of the herbs I harvest. I prefer using the electric dehydrator over simply hanging them to dry, because the process is much quicker, which means that the herbs retain more of their color and flavor. Spinach, onion and tomatoes are dehydrated for soups and pasta dishes. We still make jerky every year but have also dried potatoes, apples, zucchini chips, mushrooms, plums and watermelon. The nice thing about dried foods is that they keep for a very long time; they can be used dried or rehydrated so they are versatile, and they do not take up a lot of storage space.

Smoking is similar to drying and is the other way Native tribes preserved their food. The principle is the same as in solar dryers, electric dehydrators or ovens: warm dry air leaches the water from the food. In the case of smoking, the smoke is the warm air, and not only does it dry the food, but it also leaves behind an incredible flavor. I probably would not smoke-dry apple chips, but I would smoke-dry any meat, and smoke-dried tomatoes would be an amazing addition to a pasta sauce.

## Fermenting

Some food storage methods use things like salt and vinegar as a preservative. The two most common methods are fermentation and pickling.

Two years ago, I was co-teaching a literature class to home-schooled girls, ages 6 to 12. It focused on the American Girl series of books, which was great for the younger girls, but we decided to add a second book for the older girls so that they didn't get bored. We chose books from the Dear America series. I love history, and I especially love to read stories about people who have limited resources but manage to overcome adversity.

I was, therefore, very interested in the book about a young girl who was sent from Russia to the United States, where she was promised as a wife to a coal miner in Pennsylvania. To say life was hard for her would be an understatement, but being in America was slightly better than life in Russia had been (only slightly, though). Luckily for her, she'd learned a lot as a Russian peasant—lessons that served her well as an impoverished coal miner's wife. One lesson that had been preserved (pun, totally intended!) from her childhood was the tradition of making sauerkraut. After reading that story, I was determined to learn the technique (although in the story, the husband stomps around in a barrel of salted cabbage, and I was not really thinking we'd use that method). I did learn to make sauerkraut, however, and now one of my new favorite ways to preserve foods is through lacto-fermentation.

This method does not have the shelf life of the other storage options, but it does produce a live food that is both delicious and incredibly nutritious. Fear of food-borne illnesses have resulted in a sharp decrease in the knowledge of how to properly prepare fermented foods in a home environment, but people eat fermented foods all of the time.

For lacto-fermentation, salt is used as the preservative, but a more popular and more well-known fermented food is alcohol, which is created when the yeast (a bacteria) is given a food supply (sugar), causing it to overgrow in the liquid in which it is suspended. Most fruits and many vegetables can be fermented into alcohol. Our favorite fermented drink is hard cider and one of the ways we preserve the apple harvest.

Fermentation stops when the sugar has been completely consumed by the yeast and converted to alcohol, and at that point, the beverage needs to be bottled to cut off its exposure to air. If it continues to get exposed to air, the bacteria will start to convert the alcohol to something else, and that's actually the good news.

In the interest of reducing waste, after the apples have been peeled and cored for applesauce or juiced for cider, the leavings can be turned into apple cider vinegar. Simply fill a wide-mouthed jar with the apple peels and top with water. Cover with a cheesecloth (to keep the bugs out), and then put in a warm, dark place for about a month. After a month, strain out the apple peels and bottle the vinegar. Vinegar is an incredibly useful and healthful fermented food that a lot of people use, but most do not know enough about, and it is incredibly easy to make.

Fermented foods have a long history and are still widely used in a lot of cultures. The most well-known is sauerkraut and its Asian cousin *kimchi*, which is simply fermented cabbage. Making sauerkraut is very easy. The basic process involves slicing the cabbage very thin and then putting it in a container a little at a time, alternating with salt. The salt will draw out the water in the cabbage. A heavy object should be placed on the cabbage to keep it all below the water level. This is important because any cabbage above the water level will rot instead of fermenting, but what is below the water level can only be described as yummy. After three days of fermenting, sauerkraut can be water-bath canned to preserve it for a longer period. The canning process will give the sauerkraut a longer shelf life, but the high heat required for the boiling water bath kills the beneficial bacteria. The sauerkraut will still taste good, but will no longer be a live food. It is ready to eat in three weeks after it has been canned.

There is no comparing sauerkraut made at home to the store-bought stuff, which is often not fermented, but pickled. The home-fermented sauerkraut has a hardy robust flavor, is crunchier and tastes really good on hotdogs. Plus, in the home-fermenting environment, the amount of salt can be adjusted to taste, which makes it, overall, much healthier than what can be purchased already in a can.

## Pickling

Pickling is a very close cousin to lacto-fermentation, and since it is almost foolproof, many novice canners will choose pickling as one of their first canned foods. The high vinegar and salt content in home-canned pickles make them a pretty safe bet, too. The benefit of pickling versus lacto-fermentation is that the pickling process can take place on the same day, from harvest to sealed jar. By contrast, the lacto-fermentation process takes a few weeks. Some recipes call for soaking the cucumbers in a brine solution, at least overnight, but the recipes I use most often do not require the brine soak.

The most commonly used and most familiar pickling vegetable is a cucumber. This may be because most varieties of cucumbers are prolific growers, even (maybe, especially) when they are not particularly well tended. In fact, from my experience, the neglected cucumber vine is the one that invariably seems to do the best. Unfortunately, fresh cucumbers don't keep for very long, and there are not a lot of other options for preserving them, as cucumbers don't freeze or dry well.

## Storing Produce

Of course, some produce does not need to be cooked and sealed in jars, frozen, or dehydrated for long-term storage. Some fruits and vegetables can simply be stored in the form they are harvested. Apples, squashes/pumpkins and most root vegetables store well in cool dark places without any special equipment or preparing.

With the advent of refrigeration and our on-demand/just-in-time food delivery systems, we do not have to think about how or where to keep a winter's worth of potatoes. At the moment, most of us can simply go to the grocery store and buy more potatoes or carrots or pumpkins or apples, along with all sorts of other non-seasonal, non-storable fruits and vegetables, but that will not be the case when our food supply becomes more localized and seasonal.

While many suburban homes have basements or other storage, not all do, and in fact, of the several suburban homes I have lived in, none had a basement or garage. My current suburban home does not have a basement, a garage, a storage shed in the backyard or even a very good attic space. In fact, we don't even have very many closets, and the kitchen space could barely be considered adequate. As such, we had to find some other solutions to our food storage problem.

During the winter, we had some relatives staying with us, and one evening while we were out late, they decided to cook dinner for everyone. We received a phone call that went something like,

"If I were a potato in your house, where would I be?" My reply was, "If you were a potato in my house, you'd be in the bedroom." Followed by, "What? You don't keep potatoes in your bedroom?"

Potatoes like it cool and dark. Our bedroom is in the back part of the house, furthest away from the woodstove, which we use as our primary heat source. So, as the coldest room in the house, it served as the place where we stored our fresh vegetables. Potatoes kept for three months in a cardboard box on the floor. The long-storage apples purchased in November were starting to soften by January. The pie pumpkins and Hubbard squash stayed usable until March.

Carrots can be stored in the cool bedroom, too, but carrots and parsnips store best in sand. Lining a cardboard box with a plastic bag and then alternating between layers of slightly damp sand and carrots (or parsnips) will keep them for a good long time. Note that carrots like it cool and humid (which is why they keep well for a very long time in the refrigerator), and they don't like to touch each other.

While I did not mind so much using my bedroom as our root cellar, ultimately the plan is to build something that will allow us to store a much larger crop for longer. Our woodstove is incredibly efficient and does its job very well, which means that even the coldest room in our house was often not cold enough to be considered "cold storage." Stored better, the potatoes would have kept for six months, instead of three.

My preference would be to dig out under our house and build an honest-to-goodness root cellar, but I am concerned that digging under our house would compromise the foundation and cause our house to sag, which would be a very bad thing. The next best option would be to build a root cellar on some other part of our property, but there are several barriers to that solution, as well. The first being the septic system, which takes up a significant portion of our yard, and the second being the very limited space we have and the need to devote as much as possible to food production.

There are several very quick and easy options for storing roots outside in our small space that require only a minimum of ground space. The first option was suggested by our wizened elderly neighbor. He said we should bury a couple of barrels and layer our roots between straw. I have not tried it, yet, but it is a great idea.

My favorite solution was from the book *Root Cellaring* by Mike and Nancy Bubel. They suggest burying an old refrigerator or freezer (after removing the electrical elements on the back, of course). I love this suggestion on so many levels. The fact that it uses something that would, ordinarily, be a throw-away appliance appeals to the recycler in me. I love repurposing would-be garbage, and frankly, in the lower-energy future into which we are moving, we'll need to be doing this a lot more.

In addition, refrigerators have built-in insulation. The combination of the earth berm and the refrigerator's insulative design would keep the produce cold without freezing. In fact, it might also serve as a very good cold storage during the summer, which means we could, potentially, do away with the need for electric refrigeration.

The simplest and cheapest method is burying the produce in a pit filled with earth and straw. In my climate, where there's from one to six feet of snow on the ground at any given time from December to March, this option appeals to me the least, but in a climate where the ground isn't going to be hard frozen, this would be preferable to the store-it-on-the-floor-in-bedroom method.

We can not depend on the mega, just-in-time grocery store model we have right now to supply our food. Not only will we need to be able to grow some increasingly larger portion of our food, but we will also need to be able to preserve and store it.

Some would suggest stockpiling canned goods and five-gallon buckets of wheat and rice, and while I would never say not to buy some food for storage (heck, even I have jars and jars of beans, pasta and rice in my cabinets), I will say that when our infrastructure crumbles, and we can not just run to the grocery store when we run out, we will need to have other solutions in place. We can not make these industrial agriculture food stores the basis of our diet when there is a real threat that those sorts of foods will no longer be available. The best time to start localizing our diet is today, while we still have the support of our current on-demand food delivery system, because once the trucks stop running (and we will not know when that will be until it happens), if we don't know how to grow our own food, and we haven't started learning how to preserve and store what we have, we'll be in very bad shape.

## Easy Canning Recipes

### Applesauce

Peel, core and chop apples. Put into a large stock pot, adding sugar and cinnamon (optional) to taste. Cook until apples are soft and can be easily mashed with a spoon. We like our applesauce a little on the chunky side, which is why we peel and core the apples, but for people who like their applesauce without large pieces of apple, the apples can be simply cored (to take out the seeds), and then cooked and when soft, run through a food mill or sieve to separate the peel from the sauce.

Fill clean jars leaving a half-inch head space. Wipe off the top of the jar and fit with lids and rings. Put filled jars into the boiling water (make sure the water is at least one inch above the tops of the jars).

Boil jars for 10 minutes for pints and 15 minutes for quarts. Carefully remove jars from the hot water and let sit until cooled.

As the jars seal, there will be an audible sucking sound. Any jars that do not seal will need to be refrigerated.

### Strawberry Preserves

Wash and cut leaves from the strawberries. Put into a large stock pot, adding one half to one cup of sugar per quart of strawberries (or to taste). Let sit overnight in the refrigerator. The next day, cook the sugar/strawberry mixture until it starts to thicken and reaches the jelly stage on a candy thermometer (around 215°F).

Fill clean jars leaving a half-inch headspace. Wipe tops of jars and fit with lids and rings. Boil pint jars for 10 minutes. Carefully remove jars from the hot water and allow to sit until cooled. As the jars seal, there will be an audible sucking sound. Any jars that do not seal should be refrigerated.

One note: make sure that the tops of the jars are clean and free of any food. The jars won't seal if there is anything between the jar and the lid.

### Easy Canned Sauerkraut

Shred cabbage (carrots, beets, turnips and garlic can also be used) and tightly pack into a canning jar leaving about a half-inch of headspace (a wide-mouthed pint-sized jar works well). Add one-half teaspoon each of salt and sugar to each pint jar. Cover with boiling water and remove air bubbles. Loosely cap and allow to ferment for 24 hours. Add more boiling water leaving a half-inch headspace. Seal tightly and place in a warm place (a sunny window works well) for three days. Process in a boiling-water bath for 10 minutes for pints, 20 minutes for quarts. Allow to sit for three weeks before eating.

**DAY 7**

# Growing Food

I did not grow up in a gardening family. People who have been to my house or who know about my gardening and enthusiasm for local foods might think I grew up with a huge vegetable garden, but I didn't. The only things that grew in the front yard of the suburban home of my youth were rocks, and the only thing that grew in the backyard was the official state tree of Alabama, also known as the southern longleaf pine — the ones with those awful-to-rake pine needles, and until I was in my thirties, the only tree I could, with complete certainty, classify as a pine tree (who knew there was more than one?).

My parents never intentionally grew anything, although the first summer we lived in our suburban home, my father tried to plant grass seed. It never really took root in the sterile, pebbled soil, and three years after we moved into our house, our yard received the ugliest landscaping award from the neighborhood beautification committee — not really, because there was no ugliest yard award, although we did get lots of looks from the neighbors who couldn't understand why we didn't simply ignore the water restrictions and give our poor, brown, crinkly lawn a drink. For the entire time we lived in that house, the only intentional landscaping was the stunted bushes planted by the developer, and given how much they failed to thrive in the five years my parents owned the house, my guess would be that they were not native to the area.

I was fifteen before I had my first experience with gardening. The previous year my father had retired from his military career, and we moved to rural southeastern Kentucky, where he had grown up, and where my grandparents and most of my aunts, uncles and cousins still lived. We moved north in mid-summer and so missed most of the first year's gardening season, but my mother, determined not to miss the next gardening season, collaborated with my uncle to farm a small piece of rented land. The idea was to trade our labor for food.

As a transplanted suburban teenager, I was not quite ready to wear the will-work-for-food sign, and not only that, I had no experience with plants. No experience with plants coupled with no interest in farming equaled a great big disaster.

When we arrived at the field, which had been planted some months before and was in full bloom but in need of weeding, my uncle said, "Weed that row." To which I replied, "What's a weed?"

My uncle was not amused. In fact, given that I had been raised with a suburban work ethic (that is, work is for adults and play is for children, and for at least another three years, I was still a child, according to suburban standards) and I had a rather lackadaisical attitude toward work, in general, he thought I was just being facetious, but the fact was that, to me, all plants looked the same. They all had leaves and were green. Some of them were tall, some of them had thorns and berries, and some of them had flowers, but they were all, basically, the same to me, and I had never tried to discern any difference between one or the other.

He pointed and said, "That's a weed." So, I grabbed the plant nearest where he pointed, and he yelled at me. The plant I pulled was not the weed. It was the potato, and he let me know, in no uncertain terms, that it was a total loss. Once the potato seed has been planted, it should not be disturbed until harvest, because it can not be replanted. I had, in my ignorance (with perhaps a bit of youthful arrogance tossed in) killed his plant.

I do not recall much of what happened after that, nor whether my family was gifted any of the fresh produce from my uncle's garden. I do recall, however, that I was not asked to "help" any-more after that, and I grew to adulthood still not knowing the dif-ference between what my uncle deemed a weed and his precious potato.

In the words of the old Virginia Slims commercials, I've *come a long way, baby*, and now, not only can I tell the difference be-tween a potato and what most folks call weeds, but I can also grow football-sized potatoes in hardware cloth towers in my back yard. As such, I tend to believe that nothing is impossible. Obstacles just mean a detour is required — not that the whole trip needs to be scrapped.

When I first starting writing about staying in the suburbs and transitioning our houses and yards into small farms, there wasn't a lot of support for the idea. Again and again, what I heard was that a quarter acre was too little land, that the soil in the suburbs was sterile and nothing would grow, that restrictive homeowners' associations prohibited food production, and while these things may be true now, they don't have to be forever facts. Rules can be changed, soil can be improved, and with the right planting tech-niques, a small growing area can be made to produce enough food to feed a family, and the space can be much smaller than one would expect. In fact, one four-foot-by-four-foot garden bed can feed one adult two vegetables for the entire growing season.

What is interesting is that the longer I maintained that those obstacles were not insurmountable, the more the dissention turned to agreement, and the more I heard about people trying, even against the odds (and sometimes, blatantly flouting the rules), to become more self-sufficient on their tiny plots of land.

What I have discovered from my own experience as a suburban homesteader and from reading about others' experiences is that it can be done, and it can be done on a scale no one would have thought possible a few years ago. The key, however, is to understand that the techniques used in small-space food production are significantly different from those of farmers and gardeners with large acreages. With limited space for growing, the small-space gardener needs (to use a business term) *the highest ROI* (return on investment) possible, and in this case, the investment is mostly time and space in which the plants are grown. The return is the harvest, and in small space gardening, plants that yield a high return with a smaller investment are the ones that the suburban/urban gardener will want to plant. This means that some of the most familiar foods may need to be eliminated from our diets or be replaced by plants that we know to be food but that we do not usually eat in our typical American diet.

There are several familiar and well-loved food plants that the suburban homesteader will not want to invest time in. Corn, which is currently a staple in the American diet and is an ingredient in most processed foods, takes a large amount of space to grow in subsistence quantities. At best, in the future suburban diet, corn will be a supplemental food. In fact, most familiar grains will be supplemental, because the space needed to grow them in subsistence quantities exceeds what most suburban gardeners can spare. So, wheat, rice and corn won't be in our gardens.

Of course, without wheat (What?!? No bread?!?), corn and rice, most familiar menu items are eliminated, and the question becomes what do we grow?

The first choice for suburban self-sufficiency is trees. It might seem counterintuitive to grow trees, which would shade potential garden space, but trees are actually a great source for food, and even trees that do not seem to provide food are often some of the best to grow in small spaces.

The most obvious food trees are ones that provide fruit. There are dozens of fruit trees that work well in small spaces. In fact, most fruit trees are also available as dwarf or semi-dwarf varieties that do not grow taller than ten feet. A quarter-acre suburban yard is large enough for two standard-sized fruit trees and twice as many dwarf varieties. Further, by employing some small-space growing techniques, the suburban gardener can maximize available space. Currently we have two (mature) dwarf peach trees, one (immature) dwarf apple, a seedling dwarf cherry and plans for two more semi-dwarf apple trees that will be espaliered. Espalier is a technique in which the branches are pruned from the back and the front of the tree, and only the side branches are left to grow flat. A popular design is to plant the tree between two posts and then attach the branches (using stout cords or wire) to the posts. The tree becomes a living fence, and from anecdotal information, the trees will still produce as much as they would have if left to grow more naturally. This technique also allows trees to be planted next to walls, fences and buildings.

The type of fruit to plant depends on personal tastes and hardiness zones. With our short growing season and long cold winter, we need crops that have a long storage life. For my climate, apple trees are the best choice because they are hardy in our zone and because the fruit can be stored in a variety of ways, including fresh.

Nut trees and bushes may be an even better choice than fruit trees; they are versatile as well as valuable for their caloric density and high nutrition. Many nuts can be eaten raw. They're great roasted. Ground into butter, they're a delicious sandwich spread (think hazelnut and almond butter — not peanuts, which aren't nuts, but legumes). They go well added to salads and stir-fries. As a snack, they are probably one of the best choices. In addition, cold-pressed nuts can provide oil for a number of applications, both culinary and medicinal. Every area across North America has a native nut tree variety; wherever you live, there's probably a nut that will thrive in your neighborhood.

One tree that most suburbanites would overlook, but which is probably the most valuable nut tree, is the mighty oak. Acorns can be roasted and added to recipes for a nutty calorie-dense dish, can be coarsely ground and eaten like porridge or made into a coffee/ tea substitute, finely ground into flour and pressed for the oil. Oak trees grow in every climate in the United States, and while some acorns are better for some applications than others, with process-ing, all are edible. If we hope to grow more of our own food, we will need to grow things that are calorie dense with a high degree of nutrition. Acorns fill that need.

Of course, fruit and nut trees are not the only trees that should be considered for or included in the suburban landscape. Other trees can provide food and fuel. The most common is the maple tree, which is of great benefit for the suburban homesteader. All maple trees can be tapped to make syrup, candy and sugar. Many people believe that only the sugar maple can be tapped, and while, for commercial enterprises where efficiency is the biggest concern, this may be true, but for the home grower, if the goal is simply to have a sweetener, any maple will do. A sugar maple has a higher concentration of sugar in its sap, which means the syrup will be sweeter with less processing needed than other maple species. Keep in mind, however, that for syrup production, the maple needs to be tapped when the nights are below freezing and the days are above freezing, or the sap does not run. So, those who live in the deep South, where below-freezing temperatures are rare, trying to make maple syrup probably will not work.

In addition to the syrup, though, a maple tree is valuable as a fuel tree. Maple is a hardwood: when the properly seasoned wood is burned, the fire will be long-lasting (as opposed to soft wood fires, which burn hot and fast). Maple trees will grow from the stump of an old maple tree, which is why maple trees are often used in wood harvesting operations. As such, they can be coppiced for fuel and will regrow. For someone who only needs a bit of wood for cooking fuel or the occasional fire for heat, a maple tree is a great choice as a fuel tree.

Another tree that is useful for its sap is birch. The inner bark of the birch tree can be made into a wintergreen-flavored treat, and the tree can be tapped to make a birch syrup or beer. An interesting tidbit about birch is that the bark is probably one of the best materials for fire-making that there is. Even wet, birch bark can be used as tinder for starting a fire.

Another tree that is good for coppicing is the basswood or linden tree, and if grown only for fuel, it would be good enough, but the linden tree offers us a whole supermarket of supplies that are especially useful to homesteaders. The inner bark can be used to make amazingly strong cordage for use in tying and binding things. The flowers are medicinal and make a good tea, and the leaves are edible, like lettuce. If I could only plant one really big tree on my property, I would have a hard time choosing between the maple, the linden and the mighty oak.

Luckily, I would never have to make that choice, because my suburban lot is big enough to support all three, and at a quarter of an acre (or 10,000 square feet), my lot is a typical-sized suburban lot. Even if it were smaller, I could still plant all three trees, if I wanted. I have a neighbor whose lot is about half the size of mine (.11 acres), and she has planted thirty-plus trees and shrubs on her lot. When one starts to think in possibilities rather than limitations, the options open up.

Trees and bushes provide food but are also useful as wind-breaks and privacy, for nitrogen-fixing in soils that may have been depleted when the land was developed, for preventing erosion, for providing valuable organic mulch in the form of leaves and for providing homes for wildlife. Trees can even be used to control the temperature inside one's house. Planted on the north side of the house, trees provide a windbreak against cold northern winds. Planted on the south side of the house, trees provide shade in the summer to keep the house cool. When planted strategically on the property edges or as part of a planned edible forest garden, trees can be one of the suburban farmer's most valuable crops.

Like trees, there are many overlooked food bushes, as well. Hazelnut has traditionally been used as a hedge. It is also a great food crop. Blueberries and cranberries both grow on bushes. Blackberries and raspberries are not bushes, exactly, but are brambles, growing in some of the most inhospitable places and poorest soils, which would make them an excellent candidate for that sterile suburban dirt.

Interestingly and contrary to what most people may think, one of the benefits of suburban gardening is actually that there is limited space. While we may think this is a disadvantage, it is not. Consider that smaller gardens require fewer machines. In fact, many traditional farm machines are too large for small gardens. With the exception of a lawn mower, all of the tools we use in our gardening are manual tools.

In addition, because the space is limited, a suburban gardener is likely to have much more diverse landscape than a for-profit farmer. Most suburban gardeners want a variety of plants, which means we are less likely to create a monoculture. This diversity of plant life invites a diversity of other life (insects, birds and small mammals), which results in a whole ecosystem. The bonus is that the diverse culture is less likely to result in diseases that wipe out the entire crop. In 2009, the late blight (brought into the northeast on tomato plants grown in the south and sold by big box stores) decimated the tomato crop and damaged a good portion of the potato crop. In a permaculture/diverse plant culture suburban yard, where there is not a dependence on one food crop, losing one plant does not mean the whole season is lost. If I lose all of my tomatoes, I still have pumpkins and cabbages and apples. We might not have everything we like to eat all of the time, but we would still eat.

The last advantage has to do with the labor intensiveness of growing food. Building a raised garden bed, planting a tree and creating a forest garden can all be rather labor-intensive processes, but once the bed is built, once the tree is planted and once the forest garden is in place, *the work is done*, and all that is left to do is maintenance work and the harvest. Done properly, even the need to weed is minimized — although a better solution is to encourage weeds that can be eaten, like dandelions.

Trees and bushes are the best suburban subsistence crops, but in the interest of having a well-rounded and interesting diet, some variety will certainly be desired, and space should be devoted to perennial herbs and annuals (in raised beds and containers). Herbs are a valuable part of the suburban homestead. Many herbs are both edible and medicinal. The other benefit to adding herbs to the landscape is that purchasing them dried or fresh to be used in the kitchen can be rather expensive. In the case of herbs, DIY is always better than letting someone else grow them, because they don't take up a lot of space, and they can be grown in large enough quantities to provide for one's needs. I have been growing all of the tarragon, oregano, mint, thyme and sage that my family uses for several years. The space dedicated to growing herbs is less than 15 square feet, and they are all perennials, which means that now that they are established in my garden, the only work involved is the harvest. In addition to being useful, herbs are also very attractive, and for those who live in neighborhoods that restrict what can be grown, herbs can take the place of many of the traditional, but non-edible, landscaping plants.

Perennial edible flowers can also be used in place of traditional landscaping plants. There are many varieties of flowers that are both beautiful (for maintaining the aesthetic quality of the suburban yard) and useful as meal accompaniments. One of my daughter's favorite summer flowers is the nasturtium. All of the aerial parts of the nasturtium are edible. The flowers and leaves have a peppery flavor that adds a nice spice to salads. Cream cheese stuffed in the flowers makes a very nice appetizer. The seed pods can be picked and pickled as a substitute for capers.

The variety of edible perennial plants can be overwhelming, and unfortunately, too many of them are unfamiliar to us. My favorite recent discovery is sunchokes, or Jerusalem artichokes. Most of us are familiar with the green globe artichoke, but have no idea what a sunchoke even looks like, and further, once given the tuber, few of us would know how to prepare it.

The Jerusalem artichoke is native to the northeast. After it was introduced to Europe, it became a well-known and beloved spring tuber. In fact, it is rumored to be a favorite foraged tuber, especially among the poor. Unfortunately, that association, as a "poor man's food" resulted in the maligning of this amazing root. It produces a beautiful yellow bloom that looks like a tiny seedless sunflower growing on a stalk that can grow as tall as ten feet. They are incredibly hardy and reproduce unassisted (read: they are invasive and will take over the yard), and need almost no attention from the suburban farmer. Some people say the Jerusalem artichoke tastes like a potato, but that's like saying rabbit meat tastes like chicken. It doesn't. Rabbit tastes like rabbit, and chicken tastes like chicken, and potatoes taste like potatoes and sunchokes taste like sunchokes. The similarity to potatoes comes in the way they are prepared, and like all tubers, sunchokes are good boiled, fried and baked, but, unlike potatoes, they can also be eaten raw in a salad.

They can not, however, be harvested like potatoes. Sunchokes do not store well and need to be eaten when they are harvested (although they can be kept for a couple of days if they are kept moist), which sounds like a detriment, but isn't. Eating locally and in season means that sunchokes are a valuable food crop. In the fall, the suburban farmer harvests and stores the potatoes. By March, when the ground is thawing and the potatoes are gone, the sunchokes can be harvested and eaten, as needed. Then, over the summer, the roots left in the ground will grow and spread, while above ground, a gorgeous yellow sunflower brightens the landscape. In the fall, the plants die back, leaving the stalk so that in the spring, the tubers can be found and harvested. Whatever tubers are not harvested will grow new flowers in the summer. It's a perfect circle of subsistence, which is the ideal for the suburban homesteader.

There will be some places in the suburban yard where trees should not be planted and where raised beds should not be placed. My yard has such a place. It's called a leach field, and until I can have a composting toilet, I'm stuck with it. It takes up about a third of my usable space, and while I can't plant anything on it, that doesn't mean I can't use the space for growing food. A huge variety of plants can be grown in containers, and in fact, many varieties of fruits and vegetables have been adapted to grow well in containers. Bush beans, miniature pumpkin and watermelon vines, patio to-matoes and even corn can do well in a container garden.

Of course, containers don't have to sit on the ground. They can also hang from fences, from eaves or even from trellises. With a trellis in my front yard, I could grow the equivalent of a whole field of tomatoes and never use an inch of ground.

Plants can also be made to grow vertically. We grow potatoes in towers rather than in rows. My towers are constructed of one-inch hardware cloth, which is cheap, and easy to move from one raised bed to another. I've seen dozens of different potato tower designs from ones built out of wood with removable slats to tires. I've even seen potatoes grown in containers, like a galvanized trash can. We used a 48 gallon storage bin to grow potatoes one year, and from the three seeds we planted, we ended up with about 20 pounds of potatoes. Five pounds of seed potatoes will fill eight towers, and each tower will yield between 5 and 15 pounds of potatoes. Potato farmers know that by hilling the potatoes the yield is higher, and the potato tower design works off this fact.

## Potato Towers

*I used hardware cloth with ¼-inch squares cut into a 48-inch piece (give or take). I made a circle out of it and tied it together with a couple pieces of wire to make about a foot-and-a-half diameter circle.*

*I put "waste hay" (hay that was used as bedding in our rabbit hutches) in the very bottom, and then put seed potatoes on top of the hay and then covered the potatoes with about an inch of soil/compost from under the rabbit hutches.*

*When the potato plant was a few inches tall, I covered them with more soil, or more spent hay, or even sometimes I just used leaves that had overwintered in plastic bags, leaving about an inch of plant above the soil, and I did this until the tower was full of soil and the plant was growing out of the top.*

*I plant three to four seed potatoes per tower, usually Kennebecs because they are good storage potatoes. I need something that will store well because potatoes are a staple in our winter diet… but I only have a quarter acre to work with, and so I have to get as much as I can from a very small space.*

The suburban yard can be both beautiful and functional. Trees, herbs and flowers can add to the aesthetics of the landscape, while also providing nutrition to the homeowner. It does not have to be an either/or.

For those without homeowner association (HOA) restrictions prohibiting growing food plants and with space to devote to annual crops, the emphasis should be first on food they will eat. If family members do not like eggplant, for instance, it does not make much sense to grow it. Given the space limitations, the best choices for things to grow are things that grow fast and/or that are calorie dense.

For my climate with the need for long-storage crops, the obvious choice is root vegetables, and we devote the lion's share of our garden to growing roots like potatoes, beets, onions and garlic. The nice thing about beets, onions and garlic is the two-for-one deal. With beets, we can eat both the greens (either sautéed or raw in a salad) and the root, and the root is incredibly versatile. Beetroots can be roasted, finely chopped and used as an ingredient in chocolate cake, grated and made into sauerkraut or pickled. Onions can be harvested early and eaten as green onions or left to mature into bulbs for storage. Garlic scapes have the same familiar garlic flavor and make a delicious pesto, and garlic is a long storage root with some amazing curative powers.

The key to suburban food production is employing as many small-space gardening techniques as possible from raised beds (which have shown to be more productive when used to their fullest potential) to container gardening to hanging gardens to trellising and espalier techniques. Dozens of books provide very specific instructions on how to establish a small-space garden.

I have grown all of the garlic, onions and beets my family will use in a year in a 48-square-foot space. The key to small space food production is succession planting. Knowing when to plant is just as important as what, where and how. For instance, the general rule with regard to planting here in Maine is not to plant until Memorial Day, and for many years, I adhered to this advice religiously. Unfortunately, that meant that I never successfully grew things like beets, lettuce or peas — all of which like it a little cooler. In fact, many gardening books recommend that peas go into the ground as soon as it can be worked, which means, for me, planting almost two months before the recommended Memorial Day planting date.

I have also found that lettuce needs it colder and beets do well when planted a little early. In fact, many of the annual foods we enjoy do well in our colder climate, and so are planted earlier rather than later.

Season extension techniques are also an important consideration for the suburban farmer. Small pop-up greenhouses are a nice addition. Cold frames can be constructed out of found or re-purposed materials. If there's space and no restrictions prohibiting construction, a permanent greenhouse would not only extend the season but, using the techniques and guidance from professionals like Eliot Coleman, also provide year-round food production, even here in Maine.

For those with rigid HOA guidelines, there is no easy answer. I can not really tell anyone what to do, because I do not have to live with the consequences. The best thing those homeowners can do is to work to change the rules, but if that does not seem likely, they will have to decide if their fear of the HOA is worse than their fears of the future. In an effort to offer some hope, however, I would like to point out that, in cities across the country, individuals have succeeded in getting the rules regarding homesteading pursuits changed, specifically, the legality of keeping backyard chickens and other traditional farm animals. For those who live in communities with restrictive HOAs, my best advice is to volunteer to serve on the board, and work from the inside to get changes made.

But in the meantime, for those living with an HOA, I would strongly suggest finding edible alternatives to the traditional landscaping plants found in most suburbs. An aesthetically pleasing landscaping is the hallmark of the suburban terrain. Flowers and inedible bushes are the most common plant life, and replacing what is there can be a problem for some homeowners because there can be restrictions regarding color and size of plants. Of course, that said, a lot can be accomplished with pruning (and trees like the maple and linden that can be coppiced for fuel will not suffer from enthusiastic pruning to keep them small and within the HOA guidelines), and with a little bit of research, alternatives to the purely ornamental plants can be found.

To give some idea of the possibilities, if I lived in a Mediterranean climate, one of my choices for my edible landscape would be rosemary. It is an evergreen shrub that can grow up to six feet tall in some areas and would make a nice privacy hedge. Another evergreen bush that does not grow taller than six feet that not many people would think to use is the *camelia sinesis*. It has deep green foliage with lovely white flowers and could be a beautiful alternative to the more traditional flowering bushes with a bonus—the leaves are used to make the drink most of us know as *tea*. It is native to Asia, but is hardy in gardening zones 6 to 8. Another useful edible hedge is the American filbert, or hazelnut, which will grow in Maine, and which is currently part of my edible landscape.

There are a lot of choices for edible plants, and in fact, even some plants that are already growing in our suburban landscapes are edible (if properly processed). The problem is that time is of the essence, and starting that garden and learning about what flora can sustain us—*now*—is imperative. Once the emergency has happened, it will be too late to learn these skills. Luckily, however, there are a lot of options, but the solution will require some creativity and outside-the-box thinking.

The positive is that there are many plants that are edible, and even a few that are calorie and nutrient dense, that do not look like food, and those are the ones that suburbanites who live in restrictive areas will need to learn to grow and use. Doing so should happen now, while there is still time to make mistakes.

There are 14 days left to create our Garden of Eatin' in the suburbs. What are you waiting for?

---

*Easy seed sprouting. Take a shallow container, like a plastic sandwich keeper. Punch a small hole in the bottom. Take a tablespoon of seeds and drop them into the container. Fill it with water and allow the water to drain out of it. You should fill it with fresh water every day and let it drain. In three days or so, the seeds will start to sprout, and in four days or so, they will be ready to use as a garnish. This is really useful, especially in the winter, for adding much-needed "greens" to soups, stir-fry, sandwiches and wraps. There are a lot of uses for sprouts.*

# DAY 8

## Livestock

When most people hear the term "livestock" they automatically think about large animals, like cows and sheep and pigs. The idea that a suburban homesteader can have livestock is, therefore, ridiculous. By no stretch of the imagination is a quarter-acre lot big enough for a cow, even if that cow spends all of her time in a paddock eating store-bought hay. There would be the issue of what to do with the cow's...er, deposits, for starters, and a quarter-acre is not big enough to allow for composting cow paddies.

But livestock is not just large farm animals. "Livestock" refers to *one or more domesticated animals raised in an agricultural setting to produce commodities such as food or fiber or labor.* On a suburban subsistence homestead, livestock would be chickens, ducks, rabbits, quail and guinea hens, but could also include pigeons, guinea pigs (raised in Peru much like we raise our rabbits) and very small goats like the Nigerian dwarf or the American breed, *pygora* (a cross between a pygmy and an angora).

We have had livestock on our suburban farm almost since we bought our house, when we were given three adult rabbits — two unneutered males and an unspayed female. We did not know it at the time, but two does are actually a better ratio for raising rabbits for meat, but as we found out, one doe can still do a mighty fine job of making babies.

We, admittedly, had no idea what we were doing, and a mere eight months after acquiring our breeding stock, we had 21 rabbits. Yeah, there's that saying about breeding like rabbits, and our initial experience at being rabbit farmers was a really good reminder that most clichés have their origins in truth.

We learned that a female bunny is fertile almost from the moment she kindles. In fact, some resources I read seemed to indicate that a female can carry two litters at the same time, but this was not our experience. The gestation period for a rabbit is four weeks. Our female gave birth to three litters in about as many months, which tells me that she was fertile immediately after her babies were born, but not while she was pregnant.

Just in case anyone is wondering, no, it is not a good idea to allow a doe to kindle that close together. Having a separate hutch for the does and bucks is important. Now we know, and now we do.

The first thing most people ask when they find out that we raise rabbits for meat is what breeds we have. The answer would probably surprise a commercial breeder, but since we are not raising rabbits with the intention of selling the meat at a cost per pound, we are not necessarily as concerned about getting the most meat. In short, for the purposes of our home-raised rabbit meat, we do not need any particular breed. All rabbits are, after all, edible.

What we have found, for our own personal home use, is that a large-medium breed is actually the best. Small breeds do not have enough meat to bother (because even if raising them is easy, harvesting them is a lot of work). Large and giant breeds, which are the typical meat rabbits, require a lot more space and care than a medium breed, and so in our experience the happy medium is what works best. It is large enough to feed our family, but small enough that they do not take up as much space or need as large a hutch. It has also been our experience that the medium-sized does make better mothers, but that may have just been particular to the doe we had and not the breed.

There are dozens of rabbit breeds created for different reasons from simple pets to fiber providers to enormous meat animals. We have had all kinds. The first rabbits we raised for meat were run-of-the-mill pet store rabbits, a mix of several breeds, including lop-earreds with some long-hair or angora ancestry somewhere. They were all buff colored. When we lost our papa rabbit (that other buck I mentioned was already making his way around the circle of life), we decided to purchase a New Zealand Red breeding pair. Because he was so much bigger than our mixed doe, we decided not to breed the New Zealand buck with her, for fear that she would have trouble kindling large babies. So, she was "retired" and lived to be a pretty old girl. Unfortunately, the New Zealand doe was not a very good mother, and we only got one litter from her.

After several more unsuccessful attempts at breeding them, the New Zealand doe and buck ended up being just pets for the remainder of their lives, and when they both passed on, we just didn't have any rabbits for a few years, until I decided I wanted a fiber rabbit and purchased a purebred German angora buck. My plan was to, eventually, buy a doe and keep the breeding pair for fiber and their offspring for meat. Unfortunately, a couple of marauding neighborhood dogs cut short my plans before I could find a mate for Luigi Snowball.

As a fiber rabbit, the German angora was perfect. His pure white fur was soft and long, but German angoras need a lot of care, and an understanding of how to use clippers for shearing rabbits is probably important. Luigi was sheared once, when he was about seven months old, but his hair grew fast enough that he could have been sheared four times per year. His uncarded fur filled a one-gallon storage bag.

When we decided to get back into the rabbit business, we bought a couple of bunnies from a local feed store without knowing the gender or breed. The doe, a cross between a lop breed and probably a Himalayan, has given us several litters. She is a very good mother. The buck is a cinnamon (we like to call him Cinnamon Bun, although his name is EJ).

Our mixed-breed medium doe partnered with our large-breed cinnamon buck produces babies that give us about three pounds of meat at ten weeks of age.

The thing about having animals on suburban homesteads is that they must serve more than one purpose. When space is limited, there just is not room to be wasted, which is why I wanted to breed German angora rabbits. They would provide us meat, fiber

for spinning into yarn and, the best reason for having rabbits, fertilizer, which can be put straight into garden beds with no need to compost first. Rabbits have the most amazing manure, and the rich, healthy soil in our yard is a testament to the high nutritional quality of rabbit poo. We do not, currently, have fiber rabbits, but a nice by-product of raising rabbits for meat is their fur, which we tan to make mittens, use as a liner for moccasins or sew together for a really nice blanket. The key is to waste as little as possible. With the animals we raise for food, that means using as much of the animal as we can.

Once we (finally) decided that we weren't going to move, we started looking into other suburban livestock, and the next logical choice was chickens. In 2006, we bought our first three laying hens (after we had determined that there were no ordinances prohibiting chickens in our neighborhood). My daughters picked them from the baby chicks offered for sale at our local feed store. We also picked up all of the brooder supplies, including the wire animal cage that we still use every spring when we brood baby chicks. Unlike most people, we never did use a box as a brooder, and also unlike most people, we have always brooded the baby chicks in the house.

The benefit of brooding the future laying hens in the house is that they become incredibly tame. We lost a chicken over the winter, and then, in the spring of 2007, when we decided to expand our flock, we bought a second batch of chicks, this time a special order so that we could get specific breeds. Unfortunately, a raccoon thought our pullets were very interesting, and we ended up having to purchase pullets from the feed store. The four chickens that were not hand-raised from chicks in our brooder in the house were never as friendly as our hand-raised-from-chicks laying hens, that will allow us to walk up to them and pick them up and will even come running when we call.

Initially, we raised chickens for eggs, and they rewarded us for our efforts. Depending on the breed, a healthy, non-stressed, well-fed and watered chicken between one and three years old will lay one egg every 36 to 48 hours. Our four-year-old white leghorn lays about three eggs per week. Our year-old Light Brahmas give us one egg every day and a half.

After two years of raising laying hens, we expanded to raising meat chickens. Our goal is to raise enough chicken during our short summer so that we can eat two chickens per month for the entire year, which means we need to raise around 30 each growing season. Because we have limited space, we can only raise a dozen or so meat chickens at a time, and so we stagger the broods over the course of several months. We raise Cornish-cross chickens, because they grow really fast, reaching a weight of five pounds of dressed chicken in ten weeks, which gives our family of five three meals, if we boil the bones for broth and make soup…which we do. For the first several years of raising meat chickens, we took them to a professional and paid to have them butchered, but only because it was more convenient for us. For those who would like to raise their own meat, but are not interested in the harvest, there are specialty butchers who will dress the birds. We paid $4 per bird for butchering, but the cost was still less per pound for our hand-raised, pastured birds than what we would have paid for comparable meat at the grocery store.

By 2009, we had been raising rabbits off and on for a decade and had been chicken wranglers for three years. We decided to add ducks to our nanofarm, but not just any old ducks. Our location and limited space required that we choose our breed very carefully. Because we do not have a pond, we needed a breed that did not require water for health reasons. Our butcher will not harvest water fowl, and so we never intended to raise ducks for meat. The reason for getting ducks was for egg production, and as it happens, there is a perfect small farm breed that lays prolifically, and can live and thrive on dry land — the Khaki Campbell. Developed by a woman in England to be egg producers, the Khaki Campbell duck will, reportedly, lay better than a good laying hen. From our experience, the reports are true.

The ducks took a little longer than our chickens to start laying eggs, and, also unlike our chickens, who will give us a couple of eggs per week even on the coldest days, the ducks did not lay at all during the winter. During the warm months, each duck lays one egg every day, like clockwork. In the spring of 2010, between our three ducks and our five chickens, we were getting an average of six eggs per day. In March 2010, our birds gave us over 150 eggs.

I decided I wanted livestock in order to ensure my family's food security, but after having raised our animals for so many years, I have come to appreciate the cost savings as well.

The initial outlay for brooder supplies (cage, light fixture and heat bulb, feeder and waterer), 50 pounds of starter mash and three chicks was $100 (and please note that the small animal cage cost $60). When the chicks got a bit older, and it was time to move them outside, we spent $60 building the coop. We still use the same brooder supplies and coop, and so the only thing we pay for now, after four years of having chickens, is feed and new chicks. Feed costs us about $10 per month for six laying hens and four ducks. For our trouble, we will get around 2,000 eggs per year. Comparable eggs (but is there really anything comparable to eggs from *hand-raised, cage-free chickens and ducks?*) would cost $4 per dozen (or more for duck eggs) at the grocery store, which is $800 per year if we purchased eggs. If we wanted to be cheap and buy just eggs it would cost $400.

Baby chicks cost $2 each. Even if we bought three new hens every year, the cost to have chickens and ducks is about $126 per year, which is a savings of $274 over what we'd pay to buy cheap eggs at the grocery store, but there's one more thing that makes having chickens less expensive than buying eggs.

After our first flock of three hens started laying, we shared some of our bounty with our neighbors—a dozen different-colored eggs hand delivered in a towel-lined basket. The neighbors were so enchanted that they asked the girls to deliver eggs as often as we had extra, and for their time, the neighbors gave the girls $2 each delivery. At $2 per week for egg deliveries, the chicken feed is almost paid for each month.

To raise the meat chickens costs us about $1.50 per pound of meat. Organically raised, pastured meat birds cost between $3 and $6 per pound. Our birds are not just pasture-raised. As chicks they get the same treatment as our hens and are raised inside the house until they feather out. In addition, with such a small flock (no more than 12 at a time), they never have to compete for space, food or water, and after they're moved outside, they get all of the fresh air, sunshine, fresh grass, clean water and bugs a chicken could want.

Note: most commercial producers raise hundreds to thousands of chickens at a time, which increases stress, potential injury and the possibility of disease, prompting many producers to introduce prophylactic antibiotics. A chicken with 9 to 11 roommates does not need such measures.

One final word about our meat chickens. We chose a breed known for their size, especially their very heavy breasts, and fast growth rate. With a very finite amount of space, and a limit to the number of birds, we need them to grow very quickly. In a factory farm setting, where they also want fast-growing birds and for whom this breed was initially developed, they lose a lot of birds to physical abnormalities (such as splayed leg syndrome that causes the birds to asphyxiate when their weak legs can not support their abnormally large breasts). After several years of raising Cornish cross chicks, we have had a 100 percent success rate from brooder to butcher.

As if we did not have enough animals on our suburban homestead, we decided to add one more: bees. Of all of our livestock, the bees have had the least warm reception from our neighbors, but they are probably the most beneficial.

We wanted bees for a lot of reasons, the principal being that in trying to localize our diet and become more self-sufficient, we knew we would need to give up sugar — if at first by choice, in the end by force, when overnight, on-demand delivery of sugar was no longer available or sugar returned to being an expensive luxury item. Maple syrup is an option for an alternative sweetener, and we already tap and boil sap for syrup, but the energy requirements and the amount of sap needed for just one gallon of syrup are huge. Bees for honey seemed a more energy-efficient option.

Besides, tea and honey — yes! Tea with maple syrup...maybe not so much.

There is a plethora of information about beekeeping, and the most passionate beekeepers are more than willing to share information with the novice. In short, when we first started learning about bees, we found more information than we could easily absorb. As such, from first deciding that we did, indeed, want bees, it took another two years before we were ready to jump into the project.

The common way to keep bees is in Langstroth hives, those familiar square towers developed by an 18th-century beekeeper from Philadelphia. The benefit of using this system is that it keeps everything symmetrical and neat for the beekeeper. In addition, the shape and size of the box make them easy to move — like from a home base in Utah to an almond farm in California. Unfortunately, as with so many of the things in our society, something that works quite well on a small scale has proven not so good on the large scale, and one of the side effects of modern beekeeping has been colony collapse disorder (although the exact cause has yet to be determined and has been blamed on everything from cellphone towers to parasites to the chemicals used to spray the plants the bees are pollinating).

Some recently discovered problems of the Langstroth system include the fact that the wax used in the supers is often contaminated with pesticides or other detrimental chemicals, which means that the foundation that the bees are using for their brood comb and honeycomb is poisoning them. In addition, some research suggests that the proliferation of such parasites as the varroa mite (a particularly nasty little bug that can wipe out a bee colony) might be, if not a result of, at least exacerbated by the foundation, which uses a uniform-sized cell. Bees, in the wild, do not make all of their cells a uniform size, however, and the larval cells are actually smaller. The theory is that the larger cells take longer for the bees to close, which gives the mites an opportunity to sneak into the cell and infect the bee as it attempts to mature from larva to adult.

The beekeeper response has been to develop a different method, and after a great deal of research, we decided to use the less traditional and less well-known top-bar method of beekeeping. In choosing the top-bar hive, our hope is that we can avoid some of the problems Langstroth hive owners have experienced, and because the design does not look like a beehive, we hope that our neighbors will be more comfortable with the fact that we have stinging insects in our tiny backyard.

While our initial goal was to get honey, we are also appreciative of the fact that our bees will provide a valuable service on our nanofarm. For several years, our peach trees have had very little success in producing peaches. Part of it is because peaches need warmer weather (as with the rabbits, we can chalk it up to inexperience and ignorance, because we planted the peach trees shortly after buying our house), but also, for many years, we lived in a typical suburban environment that lacked diversity. The most prolific plant, other than native trees, was grass. Suburban grass and the indigenous trees do not provide much pollinator food, but after almost a decade of vegetable and herb gardening, we have started to notice a lot more insects in and around our yard. Our hope is that our bees will help our peaches, which will provide pollen to the bees so that they can make honey, and the end result will be home-canned peach preserves lightly sweetened with honey from our bees.

The biggest concern most people have with having bees is, of course, getting stung, and it is a valid concern, but what most people do not understand about honeybees is that they would really rather not sting. Unlike many other stinging insects, a honeybee can only sting one time, and then it dies. The other concern is with regard to swarming and the bees getting aggressive. Most domesticated bees are very docile, and when swarming, their objective is to protect the queen, who will be in the center of the swarm. Basically, the bees are not terribly interested in what humans are doing, and as long as the beekeeper offers the proper respect, he can handle the bees with a minimum of difficulty.

From the beginning, my husband decided that he was going to be as natural with the bees as possible. He opted not to have protective gear and is bare-headed and gloveless when checking the hive. He also decided against using a smoker. Many people believe that the purpose of the smoker is to make the bees calmer, but it actually has the opposite effect. Puffing smoke into the hive makes the bees believe a fire is nearby, and so they start to eat as much honey as they can. They are busy eating the honey, and, basically, ignore the beekeeper, but they are far from calm, and, in fact, are pretty freaked out. An alternative to smoke is sugar water, which is what we have chosen to use. Using a spray bottle, we spray the bees with sugar water. It does two things: first, it hinders the bees' ability to fly, and second, it gives them something to do instead of paying attention to us, which is clean the sugar water off themselves.

Not doing things like everyone else seems to be a particular quirk of ours, and we often take the road less traveled, sometimes with hilarious results. The following is my husband's account of installing the bees in our first hive.

*Today, they arrived. Wendy and the girls took a trip to Brown's Bee Farm to pick them up. Please note that we have no experience with bees, beekeeping and beehives other than a few previous stings. Also note that we desire a conscious connection with nature and all of its creatures. Said another way, we are a bit masochistic in that we did not plan to use any protective garb.*

*Boy, 10,000 bees sure do look intimidating. But...*

*So, according to the video I watched online, to install the bees:*

*Step 1: Lightly spray the bees with sugar water.*

*Piece of cake. Note: "Lightly spray" might be subjective.*

*Step 2: Remove the queen cage.*

*OK this is a little spookier…bees actually start coming out of the box. But look, isn't that nice a few bees flying around…that is, after all, why we got bees. Oh yeah, remove the plug on the bottom of the queen cage…damn, I pushed it into the cage. Wow, look, they are moving it around, and hey, one of the bees came out…OK. Now, hang it on one of the bars and put it into the hive. Cool… this seems really easy and nice.*

*Step 3: Remove the feeding can from the box.*

*OK, who designed this @ #$ɑ̃*! thing to fit so tight? Let's pry it with a screwdriver.*

*Holy cow! There are 10,000 bees in there, and now there is a big gaping hole for them to SWARM through. Quick, put the cover back on…ouch! Don't swat! Run!*

*"Little Fire Faerie, are you OK? I don't know why she stung you. I know you didn't deserve it. Wendy? No stings? Do I still have the stinger in my lip? Ouch, another one got me on the arm. OK, but we still have to finish the job."*

*Step 4: Hose them down…er, "lightly spray" one more time and then drop…bonk…the cage on the ground to wad them up in a ball, and pour them lovingly (spelled Q-U-I-C-K-L-Y) into the hive.*

*"No, forget the damned camera and help put these boards back in place when I shake the bees up and dump them into the hive."*

*"Let's go before they figure out they are free. Wow, look at that cloud of bees! Are we done? OK. Put the roof on, but, careful! Don't squash any of them."*

*Who knew that I would be initiated, welcomed even, into the world of bees. The bees have had their say and christened me properly. May we, the bees and I, develop a mutual beneficial relationship of love and trust. In spite of the fleeting moments of ~~SHEER TERROR~~ mild panic, it was a good day and I am glad to have made their acquaintance.*

We only have experience with chickens, rabbits and ducks…and we're learning about bees. For our space and our needs, those four are the best choices, but there are other options.

I know some people reading this will think *great story, but won't work for me*. Animals are not prohibited in my neighborhood, and we have outdoor space for them, but if I lived in a neighborhood, in which keeping livestock outside were prohibited, I would probably make other choices. I would still have rabbits, because many people consider rabbits to be pets, and so having them would not likely raise any eyebrows (that said, I'd have to be very careful about where I chose to butcher them, which we currently do in the backyard).

If I lived in a place where I was not allowed to have chickens and ducks, I would raise quail. They provide eggs, meat and fertilizer, just like chickens and ducks, but under certain circumstances, they would be a much better choice. One benefit to having quail rather than chickens is the space needed. One chicken needs about 2.5 square feet of space, at a minimum. In that space, six quail could be kept. The small animal cage we use as our brooder could be used to house eight to ten quail. It is 36" × 18" × 15" and has a pull-out tray so that it can be cleaned, which also means that several similar cages could be stacked one on top of the other. Six similarly sized cages with eight birds each, means that one could have 48 birds in an area that is 72 inches wide, 54 inches high and 15 inches deep. Perhaps along the wall in a garage or basement or on a balcony?

Another benefit to quail over chickens is that quail reach maturity much faster than chickens. Depending on the breed of quail, a female will start laying at about six weeks. A chicken takes six months. Of course, although they are prolific layers, quail will only lay eggs for about nine months, compared to chickens who lay (albeit unreliably after the first year) their entire life (which could be as long as a decade). The downside is that their eggs are tiny. Four quail eggs are roughly equivalent to one medium to large chicken egg.

Also, unlike chickens, quail flocks should have both male and female birds. Most suburban chicken farmers will not have roosters, because of the noise (and because chickens don't need a rooster to make eggs), but male quails do not crow. In fact, they have a lovely cricket-like chirrup when they are happy and at other times are no more loud or boisterous than the typical backyard wild bird. The positive to having both males and females is that the eggs can be fertilized and incubated, which would negate the need to purchase baby chicks every year. In fact, once the flock is established and being rotated, the only cost that needs to be associated with having quail is the feed.

If one lives in a subdivision like mine that does not currently have restrictions regarding farm animals, or like places in Oregon, where the ordinances specifically allow certain farm animals, one might consider some larger livestock, like dwarf or pygmy breeds of the larger, more traditional farm animals. Goats, pigs, cows and even horses all have small or dwarf breeds.

I have wanted goats for a long time. In an effort to be self-sufficient, and keeping with the theme of needing our animals to be multi-purpose, goats seemed the best choice for dairy animals in small spaces. Most breeds can be raised for both meat and milk (although some non-dairy breeds will not really produce very much milk, and might not be worth the trouble). Goats have also been raised for their fiber. In fact, cashmere is goat fur. My first choice for a multi-purpose goat breed is the Pygora, a cross between a pygmy and an Angora developed in the United States. It's not a great dairy breed, but is an excellent breed for fiber and meat.

Since having my own source of dairy was the primary reason for wanting goats, however, I researched other breeds and found that the Nigerian dwarf is probably a better choice. I would not have the fiber, but they are excellent for milk, which, with a very high butter fat content, would also be good for making butter and cheese.

The nice thing about small goat breeds is that they are not any bigger than a medium-sized dog. They would not need a huge space, and provided they got enough exercise (i.e., I took them for walks…like a dog), my quarter acre would probably be enough space. Unlike having a dog, however, having goats would eliminate the need for a lawnmower, as they would eat the grass…and any other plants or shrubs that got in their way.

The downside to raising goats for dairy is that they have to be bred. A goat will lactate for about nine months after kidding, at which point, she will need to be bred again if one hopes to continue getting milk. The problem is that male goats emit a really unpleasant odor when they are in rut, which would possibly cause problems with my neighbors.

Of course, there is the option of having a cow rather than a goat. A Cuban farmer has developed a dwarf dairy cow that can produce three liters of milk per day and is only three feet tall.

Both goats and cows can be dual purpose, providing milk and meat, but if one is interested in devoting space just to raise a meat animal, pot-belly and teacup pigs are smaller than some dog breeds and have enjoyed some status as pets, which might make them acceptable to the neighbors. For this suburban farmer, pork is pork.

In the very near future, space will be the only consideration for deciding which animals to keep, as zoning is changed to allow for food production in urban and suburban areas, but until then, homeowners who live in restricted areas will need to comply with the laws, while not sacrificing their family's future, which means getting creative with "pets."

Some non-traditional choices would likely not raise eyebrows, at least initially, like the already mentioned quail; in the Peruvian mountains, guinea pigs are raised in much the same way that American homesteaders and farmers raise rabbits. While some more restrictive homeowner's associations will ban rabbits, guinea pigs are not against the rules.

Finally, there is always the option of just ignoring the rules. In a very long discussion once upon a time, I said that if I lived in a 2,500 or 3,000 square-foot house with a garage and a basement, I would find room for my animals inside the house. There are a lot of issues involving this choice, and there has to be the willingness, on the homeowner's part, to accept the consequences of flouting the law, but it can be done. We brood chicks inside our house every spring. They live in a standard-sized small animal cage on the carpeted floor of my office until they are fully feathered and they can survive outside. Then we transition the pullets into the laying flock and the broilers into a chicken tractor outside until they are ready to go to the butcher. If I could not keep them outside, I would find a larger area inside my house for them to live, and if I had a garage or a basement, I would not think twice about setting up an area there for them — complete with several interchangeable trays in which I would grow sprouts for them to peck and forage (because chickens who have access to greens are much happier).

In his book, *Omnivore's Dilemma*, Michael Pollan describes his visit to Joel Salatin's Polyface Farm. Salatin's son raises rabbits in a shed. Having raised rabbits, I know that it is ideal to have them in a wide-open and well ventilated area, because rabbits can be rather...ahem...*aromatic*. What Pollan observed, however, was that the rabbits kept in this small closed space did not have any offensive odor, and it was because of Salatin's practice of cooperative husbandry techniques. In that same shed with the rabbits, Salatin's son was also keeping chickens, who lived under the rabbit cages and scratched around in the litter. The two animals, housed together, kept things from getting unpleasant. Salatin's son, of course, had a great deal of responsibility to keep the area clean, as well, but even the most attentive farmer would have had difficulty keeping that small closed space habitable, if not for the chickens' help. Rabbits and chickens can be kept quite successfully in a suburban basement or garage with few problems, and using the cooperative farming techniques pioneered by Salatin at Polyface Farm, even we small-space homesteaders can provide a good portion of our own food needs.

Getting started does not take a lot of time or money, but with only 13 days left, the best time to start is now.

## The Chick House

Before beginning my foray into chicken ownership, I spent some time researching what I was getting into. Barbara Kilarski's book, *Keep Chickens*, was a wonderful resource for everything from choosing a breed to the size of their enclosure. While my hope was that they would be able to also spend some time free-ranging around the yard, my plan was to build the coop big enough that they could spend all of their time in there, if they had to.

We only have a quarter acre of land, and while our neighbors have a half acre and an acre respectively, I didn't wish to push my luck by letting my chickens loose to roam in their yards. They probably wouldn't care, but as Frost's neighbor observed in the "Mending Wall," "good fences make good neighbors," and as there are fences, it is probably best that I keep "mine" on this side of them.

In addition, with only a quarter acre, space is a premium, and none can be wasted or under-utilized. Every side of my house has some edible plant or planting bed, especially the south-facing backyard. Chickens can really wreak havoc in a newly planted garden bed. They like to scratch things, and soft, newly planted soil with tasty little seedlings is too much to pass up. Not to mention that, with several feet of snow on the ground, I knew the chickens would not be doing much "free ranging," and so they would likely spend at least four months cooped up. The first requirement, therefore, was that it be large enough to allow the chickens room to spread their wings.

Kilarski's book gave me the basic dimensions we needed to ensure that the chickens had enough room, but I spent some time online looking at different designs. We had just come out of a pretty harsh winter. Our driveway is not big enough to plow, and

so it must be shoveled. In addition to the driveway, roughly the size of two large parking spaces, we shovel a path from the road back to the oil and propane tanks. Since moving here, we have had rabbits, and so we have always had to shovel a path back to the rabbit cages. Plus, at some point, the snow just gets too deep for our dogs to squat anymore, and we will usually help them out by shoveling a little place for them to take care of their business. Snow. It's a real thing here.

I knew that my chicken run would have to be covered, because there was no way I was going to be shoveling it out. Thus, the second requirement was that it have a roof of some sort — something to keep out the snow and to protect the chickens from the rain.

I am not very handy. I can drive in a nail or screw in a screw. I can even drill a hole, but...suffice it to say that I am a "helper" when it comes to construction, and not a very strong one of those. So, I needed my husband's help with building the coop. The problem was that he was still mad about the fact that we had chickens at all. *We* had never agreed to chickens. They just came home with me one day...from the feed store, and they brought all of the things they would need to be comfortable — a brooder cage, lights, water dishes, feed dishes, feed. He was not happy. To compound matters, I do not control the purse strings, and so, not only was he being forced to build a coop for chickens he never wanted, but he was also going to have to figure out what needed to be bought *and* then pay for it. Oh, he was seriously *not* happy. The third requirement was that it be cheap and use as many of the various pieces as possible of construction flotsam and jetsam we had lying around the yard from previous projects.

The additional complication was that our "original" design, which I dubbed the "Frankenstein Coop," was decent at keeping the chickens *in*, but poor at keeping critters out. As such, we lost our best laying hen and three pullets to a raccoon. That was tough and necessitated another trip to the feed store for more chickens. As such, the fourth requirement was that our coop be "predator proof."

A final consideration in our coop design was that it be tall enough that we could walk into it and open enough that my children could go in there and hang out with the chickens, which they like to do. With all of those requirements in mind, first we sketched a couple of potential designs. We agreed on a basic framework and got to work.

We constructed the roof of the Frankenstein Coop using four eight-foot two-by-fours, attaching two together with screws on one end to make two Vs that we attached together using one-by-twos. Then we took some corrugated clear plastic roofing and screwed it down on the frame. The roof has a 30° pitch and, when it's sitting on the ground, is about four feet at its peak.

For the sides, we used the top and bottom frames, roughly eight feet long and two feet wide, from an old rabbit hutch we had built inside of our once-upon-a-time shed that the Town made us get rid of. With the roof attached to the side frames, the peak is about six feet, tapering down to two feet.

The rest of the coop design was, basically, dictated by the side pieces and the roof. With purchased two-by-fours, we made the back and front walls and the door. We also purchased 50 feet of 48-inch chicken wire and stapled it to the frame all around. Pieces of six-inch plastic garden edging hammered into the ground deterred digging predators.

Inside the coop, a remodeled rabbit hutch is the hen house. We replaced the front wire with bottom-hinging doors and replaced the wire floor with a piece of plywood. Because we had to cut off the legs to fit it into the coop, the "house" is only a foot or so off of the ground, but this works out pretty well, because the "doors" also serve as a sort of "chicken ladder." When the "ladies" are ready to go to bed at night, they walk up the "door" and into their house. Then, we close and latch the doors until morning.

Inside the house are four nesting boxes, and the front frame of each nesting box is a roosting bar. The house is roughly seven feet wide by four feet deep and three feet tall on the inside. The hens roost about a foot up from the floor of the house.

The only real drawback of our house design is that the hens roost right above the nesting boxes, and chickens poop…a *lot*, which means the nesting boxes get full of poop. But the hens have figured out a solution — they nest on one side of the house and roost on the other. That way, one nesting box, which they all use, is clean and poop free for laying eggs. Based on this observation alone, I disagree with the assertion that chickens are stupid, and with the claim that they are "nasty" or "dirty." They apparently do not enjoy sitting in poop to lay their eggs.

The only real drawback of the "run" design is that the hens can get under the house and back behind it, and then we can not reach them. So, far, it has not been an issue.

As luck would have it, our coop design was pretty ingenious. Our backyard is on the southern side of our property. We put the coop in the southwestern-most corner of the backyard. In the summer when we built it, it was under the trees, in the shade, which kept the chickens out of the sun and kept them cool. That part of our property is all deciduous trees;as a result, during the winter, the coop gets full sun all day.

The walls are just a two-by-four frame with a wire covering. For years, we have housed rabbits outside all year long, and they have always been just fine. In the winter, we wrap any open parts of their hutches with clear plastic sheathing. We did the same for our chickens. The plastic-wrapped walls combined with the clear plastic roof and the full day of sun resulted in the ground inside in the coop never freezing—all winter, even when we had weeks of sub-zero nights and below-freezing days. On some nights, the water would freeze, but the hens would be snug inside their 96 cubic feet, where their bodies would keep each other warm. During the day, when the sun came up, they stayed cozy inside the coop, and on particularly sunny days, the inside temperature of the coop would be as much as 20° warmer than outside the coop.

And they could still scratch around on the ground, because the floor of their run is just straw-covered dirt that never froze. Because it was all enclosed, we never had to shovel, either, although, as with the rabbits, we did have to shovel a path back to the coop, and a couple of times, we had to chip the ice in front of the door so that we could open it.

The final bonus to our coop design was that our chickens continued to lay all winter. We believe it was the combination of natural light and the daytime warmth of the coop. In fact, they gave us an average of four eggs per day, all winter, with the oldest hen, Penny, in the middle of her molt in December.

We do not have any electricity in our coop. Being a small hen house, it is heated with just the chickens' own body heat and the solar heating of the coop during the day; no lights or heaters are needed.

Before we built our coop, I spent exhaustive hours scouring the Internet for ideas, and even thought I wanted to buy a kit or a prefab coop, but in the end, with the desire to be frugal paramount, what we built was almost divinely inspired...and probably saved us about $150.

And as for my husband, I believe he has finally made his peace with the chickens. He even feeds them in the morning and tucks them in at night.

DAY 9

Laundry

Sometime in the spring of 2008, I got roped into watching the television series *Grey's Anatomy* on DVD while my daughters were in their dance classes. I no longer watch television, and we were starting with season one when the program was in its fifth season.

In one of the episodes, one of the young interns is intimately involved with one of the doctors, who is completely anal-retentive, from his attention to detail in the operating room (a good trait in a doctor) to his obsessive neatness. His love interest, while his anal-retentive equal in the operating room, is the *yang* to his *yin* when it comes to being tidy. She's a slob, and when he asks her to move in with him, she tells him, "I don't do laundry. I buy new underwear."

It is funny coming from a fictitious character in a prime-time soap opera, but it's not a reality that most of us experience. At some point, most of us real-life people do "do laundry," and if we have families and children, we do "do" a *lot* of laundry. In a lower-energy future, we will probably have less laundry, because we will simply have fewer pieces of clothing, but less does not mean none, and if we have fewer clothes, we will really need to take good care of the ones we have, which means keeping them clean and mended.

In our modern households, we all have washing machines, and frankly, of all of the modern conveniences, I can think of only one or two other appliances I will be sadder to see gone than my washing machine. I can (and do) happily survive without the electric dryer, but I do so love the washing machine.

Of course, if we do not have electricity or our supply is limited, I am not going to waste precious power agitating my clothes with a machine, when I can do it just as well by hand.

The laundry chore has come a long way in the past hundred years. Now, we have super energy-efficient, superior cleaning front-end loading machines that can clean the smile off the Cheshire cat. I still have a top-loading dinosaur. My grandmother was lucky enough to have an electric wringer washer, but not that long ago,

washing laundry in a tub and wringing with a hand-crank wringer was pretty high-tech.

I was very lucky in that some relatives who enjoy antiquing learned that I wanted one of those old-fashioned wringers. They had displayed one with their other "antique" tools and probably thought I wanted it as a novelty item, but the truth is much more bizarre. I planned to use it…not every day, but in the event of a total collapse, I wanted to be as prepared in as many areas as possible. So, they found one for me, and I paid $50 for this amazingly well-preserved antique.

I also have a 16-gallon galvanized washtub, and in December 2008, when the Northeast was hit with a severe ice storm that knocked out power for four days, I had the opportunity try out my new toys.

With water heated on the woodstove, we used the washtub for bathing. After our baths, I threw a load of clothes into the water, and using the grape-stomping technique, I agitated them. Then, I used my wringer (and let me just say that it was some hard work wringing out those clothes, and that I now truly understand how easy we have it when it comes to doing laundry…and why people didn't want so many clothes back before the electric washing machine was invented). After washing and wringing out the clothes, I hung them on the line outside — yes, in the winter. It was a gorgeous, sunny day with a steady light wind, and it did not take long for them to dry.

There are some practical benefits to doing laundry the low-tech way. Handwashing is much more gentle on clothes than the machine, which is why so many fragile clothing items recommend hand laundering. Even using my crank-powered wringer is more gentle than the electric-powered spinning tub action of my washing machine (except with regard to buttons, and one should be very careful when threading fragile buttons through the wringer).

Using a clothesline instead of a dryer also increases the life expectancy of clothes exponentially. The high heat of the average dryer does more to break down the fabric fibers than even the roughest of rowdy children.

Line-drying clothes has other benefits not matched by the dryer, as well. Hanging clothes in the sun bleaches them, which, unfortunately fades bright colors after a time, but it also whitens whites without the use of harsh chemicals. Line-drying clothes gives them a fresher smell without the use of chemical (and potentially hazardous) fabric softeners. Adding a little vinegar to the rinse water will keep line-dried clothes from getting stiff, and a little essential oil added to the rinse water will give the clothes a perfumed smell, if one desires it. On windy days, my clothes dry faster outside than in the dryer and smell much nicer, too. Line placement plays a big part in how quickly the clothes dry, and I would recommend placing the line in a sunny spot away from buildings and fences that might obstruct airflow.

I have a washtub, and I could add a washboard to be sure that my clothes were really getting clean. I could just as easily do my laundry in the bathtub or a bucket. I used the stomp method, but I have also seen the plunger method, where a clean plunger is used to agitate the clothes. Another option is to invest in a Wonder Wash, which is a plastic tub with an airlock lid on a pedestal. The clothes, water and detergent are placed in the container, the airlock lid is fitted into place, and then the whole thing is spun using a little handle. The gyrating action agitates the clothes cleaning them. The Wonder Wash is great for small loads, but for a family like mine, with lots of clothes, and lots of heavy clothes like towels and blue jeans, it would require doing several very small loads at a time.

Another low-tech (albeit incredibly expensive) option is the antique James Washer. Basically, it is a rectangular washtub with a plug at one end and a handle on the other. The tub is set into a frame that allows the tub to swing, and when it has been filled with clothes and water, the handle is used to agitate the clothes. It can be fitted, for an additional cost, with a wringer, and it is a nice all-in-one option for someone who has hundreds of dollars to invest, but the key is that the James Washer will likely outlive most of us (and, thus, be worth the money spent), unlike the modern Wonder Wash, which is manufactured using cheap plastic.

Of course, for those who do not have the money to spend on the James Washer or the Wonder Wash, there are some low-tech solutions that simply require a bit of creativity. The one thing all of the washers have in common is that they do the agitation with very little human energy required. Spinning a handle is slightly less physically taxing than grape stomping the clothes or than agitating the clothes with a plunger, but it is also true that our leg muscles, whether we are male or female, are more powerful than our arm muscles, and there are some creative DIY washer solutions with that in mind.

For the mechanically inclined, there is the bicycle-powered agitator. Using an electric washing machine configuration and an old bicycle, one can rig up a pulley system so that the washtub is agitated and spun using the bicycle to do the work. A regular washing machine tub, when full of water and wet clothes is incredibly heavy, even under the best of circumstances, however, which explains why the washer motors often burn out, and operating this sort of washing machine can be physically taxing for the average person.

Another option is the rocker method, suggested by blogger Jim Dakin, in which a regular washtub is fixed to the seat of an old rocking chair. Fill the tub with clothes, water and detergent, and then push back and forth on the rungs of the chair to produce the agitation necessary to clean the clothes. For the wringer portion, the suggestion is to invest in a mop-bucket wringer, like those used by the school janitor (or anyone who has ever worked in the fast-food industry) and available at most hardware stores. A mop is not quite as thin as the average piece of clothing, but the bulk of the water would be removed, which would ensure faster drying. In addition, anyone who has ever tried to hand-wring clothes knows that it is difficult and will appreciate anything that makes getting water out of the clothes easier.

Many creative solutions can be developed, but whatever the method used, it is wise to have a plan for tackling the laundry issue, because several days into the emergency, when things start to settle and routines start being established, there is going to be a pile of potentially ripening clothes that need to be cleaned.

Once the washing method is figured out, the next step is to decide on what will clean the clothes, which means soap. Stockpiling laundry detergent from the grocery store is one option, and if one ignores some of the more frightening information about the health risks associated with using commercial detergents, then having cases of Tide detergent on the basement shelf is certainly better than nothing.

Of course, with any supplies, the better idea is to stock "ingredients" that can be used in a variety of applications. A simple homemade laundry soap uses washing powder, borax, baking soda and any bar of soap—all of which can be used in other cleaning applications (unlike Tide, which is just for fabrics).

## Homemade Laundry Soap

*2 cups grated bar soap*
*1 cup washing soda*
*1 cup baking soda*
*1 cup borax powder*
*Mix all ingredients well. Store in an airtight container.*
*Use 1/8 to 1/5 cup per wash load.*

I love the idea of homemade soap, and in fact, we use a 1:1 mixture of washing soda and borax for dishwashing. My problem with it is that there may come a day when washing soda and borax powder simply are not available, and then what? The answer is to make lye soap, which sounds really awful, because everyone knows that lye is caustic and dangerous and can cause serious injury if handled improperly. Lye *soap* (not the lye itself, which is caustic and dangerous and can cause serious injury if handled improperly) is actually gentler than most commercial soaps. The lye is bad, but when boiled with animal fat the chemical reaction, called *saponification*, produces glycerol and a fatty acid salt…or soap. Chemistry is so cool.

Our ancestors regularly made lye soap using the following method. The first step is to make the lye. Lye is also called potash, and the chemical name is potassium hydroxide (and for the real chemistry geek, like my husband, the symbol is KOH). Lye or potash is made by filtering soft water (like rainwater) through hardwood ashes. It is important to use hardwood and not softwood, as the quality of the lye will not be as good if softwood (like pine) is used. Of course, I say, use what you got.

In Colonial times, a special apparatus was constructed to make the lye, but the simplest method uses a clay pot with a hole in the bottom. Place a layer of hay on the bottom to keep the ash in the container and not in the filtered water. Then fill the pot with wood ashes (probably ones that are not hot anymore would be best). Pour water, a gallon at a time, through the ashes and allow it to seep into a non-metallic bucket (aluminum, especially, will react to the lye, and should never be used in soap-making if lye is being used).

To make a stronger lye, after several gallons of water have been filtered through the ash, some resources recommend boiling most of the water off, but a stronger lye will only mean that the resulting soap hardens into bars. A weaker lye still makes soap; it will just be liquid. Other sources recommend filtering the lye water through the ash several times to make the lye stronger.

The second ingredient in soap-making is rendered animal fat. In Colonial times, either tallow (beef fat) or lard (pig fat) was used, but any animal fat will do. In fact, raccoon fat makes a suitable soap—not that I recommend going out and killing raccoons just to get fat for the soap, but if said raccoon was killing the chickens, I say he is fair game, and at least at my house, his remains will be put to good use (eat my chickens, I eat you—eye for an eye and all). Of course, instead of just killing the creature and then throwing away the carcass, it would be better to use as much of the animal as possible so that his death is not merely an act of vengeance. An integral part of homesteading is using all of the gifts we are given.

In Colonial times, soap-making was a combination of experience, hope and magic, typically with new soap-makers hoping that they could magic a useful product by paying special attention to the moon's position on the horizon and whether or not the caterpillars were aligned. Of course experienced soap-makers often had the same problem. There was no written recipe, and winging it was normal. In addition, they had very little understanding of the chemistry involved. They knew what happened when lye was mixed with water and then animal fat, but not why.

Luckily for us, dozens of recipes for making lye soap are in books and on the Internet. Most use a stronger, commercial lye product than I would use (because boiling down gallons and gallons of caustic water simply does not appeal to me, and because if the goal is self-sufficiency then relying on a purchased product for half of my ingredients does not make a lot of sense. If it did, I would just use borax and soda ash, right?).

After the lye is made and the fat is rendered, the next step is to mix the lye and fat together, which will create the desired saponification, i.e., make soap. Essential oils can be added to make it smell prettier, if one wishes.

## Basic Lye Soap

*1 cup of cold distilled water*
*2 tablespoons lye*
*1 cup animal fat*
*Carefully pour the lye into the water, not the other way around though, and stir. The lye will heat up the water. Allow to cool.*
*Melt the animal fat. Allow to cool.*
*When both the lye water and animal fat have reached about the same temperature, between 100° and 110°, carefully pour the fat into the lye water, stirring constantly.*
*Continue stirring until the mixture starts to thicken (from 20 minutes to an hour) and lines, or "trailings," are observed on the surface.*
*\*\*Note: If trailings aren't seen within four hours, it's probably a lost cause, and I'd start over from the beginning.*
*Carefully pour the soap mixture into a mold, cover and allow to sit for 48 hours to harden. When the soap is firm, it can be cut into bars.*
*\*Makes about a ½ pound of soap, which isn't a lot, but is a good place to start.*

There are a lot of things that can go wrong with making soap, and the only way to learn is to do it…often. In Colonial times, the hit-or-miss soap-making usually resulted in a liquid soap, but commercial soap-makers would add salt to make bars. Soft soap works just as well for cleaning as bar soap, and salt was a very precious commodity and needed for preserving food. As such, most Colonial households just used the liquid soap. As long as the soap does not curdle or the fat does not separate out, it will be okay for use as a liquid, especially for laundry.

For the most part, making soap requires nothing that the average suburbanite can not acquire. The baking aisle of the grocery store sells lard. Be sure that it is lard, though, i.e., animal fat, and none of that crappy, pseudo-good-for-you, chemically processed, partially hydrogenated-vegetable shortening. Better yet, finding a local butcher (like the one who processes the backyard chickens) who can supply some beef or pig fat, which can be rendered into lard, would probably be the best option.

And remember that it is better to have on hand *ingredients* than it is to have the whole products, because it takes a lot less space to store the amount of lard needed to make hundreds of batches of soap than it does to store an equal amount of laundry detergent.

Plus, lye soap can be used to wash bodies, too. Tide can not… or at least it shouldn't be.

We have 12 more days. It is worthwhile to make some plans on how to keep those clothes from standing up in the corner by themselves.

## Resources

Colonial Soap-making: alcasoft.com/soapfact/history.html
Lye-making: lifeunplugged.net/everythingelse/make-lye-from
-wood-ash.aspx

**DAY 10**

# Lights

One thing I will never figure out is why my daughter loves power outages. She is very much a product of our modern world, as are we all, and enjoys all things electronic, especially anything that has entertainment value, like movies and playing on the computer. When there is no electricity, however, she can not enjoy these activities.

Further, she hates the dark. Like many people, especially children but also a fair number of adults, she fears that there is something "out there...in the dark" that might cause her harm, and so while she professes to enjoy not having electricity, the truth is that it is fun during the day trying to find creative ways to entertain herself, but once the sun goes down (or on overcast days), she is ready for the electricity to come back on.

What is unfortunate is that lights are probably the least useful of all things electric. It is true that having lights allows us to work longer and do more at night, and they are especially wonderful during the winter when, at least where I live, days are very short (lasting only about eight hours around the winter solstice). Without light, we are extremely limited in what we could accomplish when the days get very short, and face it, as much as I like sleeping, I am not likely to go to bed at 4:00 PM and sleep until 7:00 AM.

Human beings need light to see. Unlike cats, whose eyes are designed to see clearly in very low light (cats actually can not see any better than us in total darkness — they do need some amount of light to see, just not much), we need a fair amount of light to accomplish precision tasks. Things like reading, especially as we get older, are very difficult to accomplish in low light. In a lower-energy society, we are going to have low light at night; however, even low light is better than no light.

So, what are our options? The most obvious answer is candles. Who does not love the ambience of a candlelit room? When I was younger, I had a friend who said that everyone looked better by candlelight, because the glow of the candles rendered one's skin an amber color. Perhaps that is why candles are so romantic.

In Feng Shui, candles hold a significant place in harnessing positive energy. Burning nine candles brings good vibes to one's house, and it looks pretty cool, too.

Today, candles come in all sizes and styles and are often scented. Most of them are also petroleum-based, and as we continue to experience a decrease in the amount of available oil, we may also find that the availability of Yankee candles is diminished. As such, making our candles will, likely, be something we will want to know how to do.

There are two types of candle-making: poured candles and dipped candles. With the first method, melted wax is poured into a mold and a wick, often made of a cotton fiber, is inserted and then allowed to dry. With dipped candles, a wick is attached to some kind of holder (we attach our wick to a stick) and slowly lowered into the melted wax until it is coated. It is taken out, and the wax is allowed to cool slightly (this only takes a couple of seconds), and the process is repeated until the desired thickness is achieved.

Both methods take a fair amount of time when done in a home setting without fancy automated equipment. With the poured candle, the time-consuming part is just waiting for the wax to harden, which can take a very long time. With the dipped candles, it is the dipping and waiting, and dipping and waiting. Of course, if children are involved, dipping candles can actually be a lot of fun, and involving them in projects that will empower them to be more self-sufficient in a lower-energy future is not a bad thing.

At the moment, finding petro-wax candles is only a matter of going to the closest grocery store. Mine has half an aisle devoted to scented candles. Some stores sell only candles and candle accessories, like little lanterns for burning tea lights, etc.

I enjoy using candles. The part I never enjoyed was having a half-inch of leftover candle that would not burn. So, I started to save these little wax discs. Initially, I was using them to make fire starters. Then, I learned how to build a fire properly, and I no longer needed a fire starter, but I could not throw away the wax discs. Now I use them in making dipped candles with my children. In a lower-energy future, there will be no room for waste, and recycling, reusing and reducing have become very much the way my family lives our lives.

Most commercial candles, especially the scented ones, are made using a petrochemical derivative, which will be scarce in a low-energy future. Earlier, beeswax was used to make candles, and it does a nice job. Unfortunately, unless one has bees, acquiring beeswax may be a challenge. My rather flippant advice is to get bees, but of course, I realize that may not be an option for many people, and other things have been used to make candles, such as animal fat. If we think about it, we have heard about tallow candles, although many of us may not really know what they are. Tallow, the rendered fat of large hoofed animals like cows, is used in candle-making and soap-making. Just be aware that tallow candles tend to be a little messier than wax candles.

Unfortunately, candles do not give off a great deal of light. One way to get the candle to glow a little brighter is to put it in front of mirrors or other reflective surfaces. We have all seen the candle holders with what looks like a pie plate attached, the idea being that it will reflect the candlelight making it more intense. We have found this to be the case, and in addition to putting mirrors behind candles, we also have mirror tiles under candles on our table. They reflect the light and catch the wax, which is much easier to clean off mirrors than it is to clean off a wooden table.

Even with reflecting the light from candles to make it brighter, if I knew that I would never again have electric lights, I would want something else, too. In this case, our oil lamps work very well. In these modern times, petroleum-based kerosene is most often used in oil lamps, but it has some significant disadvantages. It is a petro-fuel, which is likely to become very scarce and/or very costly. The question is, if we can not use kerosene, what can we use? I would ask what people used before there was kerosene, and the answer is oil... like what we know as cooking oil, with olive oil being the most well-known. Think Aladdin and the story with the genie in the lamp. How many people fully grasp the fact that the genie's lamp was an oil lamp, and if the genie had not been living in it, it would have been used by Aladdin for light? The vessel of the lamp held the oil, and the spout held the wick. As in our modern kerosene lamps, the wick was drenched in oil, which caused it to burn slowly and provide light.

There are some distinct advantages to using olive oil over kerosene. While it is a great fuel for cooking and for lighting, if the lamp is toppled, the oil will not catch fire like kerosene will, which makes olive oil a much safer fuel. In fact, a lit match dropped it into a bowl of olive oil would merely sputter out, as we saw. Try that with kerosene and be prepared to call 911 — assuming one is still able to call 911.

Other organic oils are similar to olive oil. In parts of the world where olives are not grown, but fuel for lighting was desired, animal fats were often used. Like olive oil, they will burn, but if the vessel is capsized, the fat will douse the flame rather than igniting and causing a bigger problem. Many tribes indigenous to North America are said to have burned bear fat for light. Raccoon fat, which does not solidify like cow fat (tallow), is good for rendering to be used in oil lamps, and believe it or not, we have actually used it as a fuel for lighting.

The third disadvantage to using kerosene is pollution. As we transition from a consumptive lifestyle, this will not be such a problem, but there is significant research to suggest that indoor pollution is equal to or worse than outdoor pollution. Burning organic fuels, like olive oil and animal fats, does not produce the same toxic and potentially carcinogenic fumes that burning petro-fuels produces (incidentally, those lovely, scented petro-wax candles are also very polluting).

High-tech options for lighting, such as CFL and LED bulbs, require only a very small amount of electricity, much of which can be stored in batteries from a solar generation system. Solar-powered lamps and solar garden lighting store power from the sun during the day and use that energy to power a dim light at night. The light is not much more than what is provided with a candle, however, and as with my camp lantern, if I did not already have the solar lights, I would not invest the money in them. Candles, or better wax and wicks for making candles (remember, storing ingredients takes up less space), are far less costly and are infinitely more efficient in the long-term.

The problem with high-tech lighting is that, at some point, something will fail. No engine or electronic device is made to last forever, especially with built-in and planned obsolescence: wires break, light bulbs burn out, capacitors fizzle, resistors stop resisting.

We have few options for low-energy lighting. As much as I love my camp lantern (the light is very bright compared to other types of low-energy lighting), because it depends on electricity to charge, it is not something I would recommend buying. Instead I would suggest buying an oil lantern or the materials to make candles. I do plan to use my lantern as long as I can, but at some point, I know the spark will die, and I will have no way to revive it.

We have 11 more days, and if sitting in the dark does not sound especially appealing, it might be a good idea to start practicing dipping or molding…or checking out the oil lamps. The Genie is not likely to pop out and grant the wish for life to go on unchanged, but filled with oil, the lamp could still beat back the darkness, even if just a little.

# DAY 11

## Electricity

I will admit that we like having electricity. In fact, I think I already have — admitted it, that is. For many of the items used on a daily basis, like the computer on which I am typing this manuscript, there is simply no substitute for electricity. Most alternatives to the computer do not really compare, even just for typing (or word processing, as it is called in computer lingo).

Still, the fact remains that we *can* live without electricity. First, think of all of the things we have in our homes that require electricity, and then try to imagine how that same task can be accomplished without the electrical appliance. I have or will talk about the low-energy alternatives to washing machines and dryers, heating, cooking and lighting. Instead of watching television, we can learn to play music, read a book, play games or perform dramatic presentations. For most of what electricity provides us, there are better non-electric alternatives, and in fact, people managed to survive and thrive without electric lights and laptop computers for millions of years, and that really is what we have to remember.

Still, I like having my computer. Typing is easier on the computer, for instance, but more importantly it serves as a fantastic information storage device for all of my journals, rough drafts of stories, my daughters' home-schooling history, and years' worth of digital family photos. My parents had hundreds of vinyl LPs and cassettes with all of their music. Mine is all on my computer in one easy-to-locate place. If we're very lucky in a low-energy future, we might still even be able to use the computer as a communication device. In short, it would be nice to have the computer for a while, even if the grid goes down.

In a lower-energy future, if we want to have electricity for things like our laptops and freezers, we will need to be able to generate some portion of it ourselves. Unfortunately, we have been led to believe that doing so is difficult and costly. It does not have to be either.

The most common way people know to generate electricity on an individual level is by using solar power. A whole industry has grown up around the development of solar power generation equipment, and in fact, solar panels can be found for nearly every application from a simple backpack to a whole house array. We have dozens of pieces of solar paraphernalia: flashlights, iPod charger/speaker, radios, simple battery chargers. I love our solar stuff, and at some point, I will probably get more of it. In fact, I would love to have a small photovoltaic (PV) system that is at least big enough to power all of our computers and peripherals and the freezer.

The problem with depending on solar systems, however, is that propensity for many of us to think that technology will save us. Solar generation equipment is an amazing technological feat that was only possible because of cheap oil. They can not be manufactured easily or inexpensively (and make no mistake, today's prices for solar gadgets are incredibly cheaper than just a few years ago)

without massive power inputs that use fossil fuels. Even the lab-
oratories where engineers conceive of these modern marvels are
powered with fossil fuels, and seriously, if anyone knows where I
can find a PV system that was manufactured using solar power, let
me know. I'd love to buy it, but I suspect it doesn't exist.

An alternative to solar power is wind generation equipment.
Today's windmills are nothing like those Don Quixote fought.
They are smaller and quieter and infinitely more efficient. Like
solar power generation systems, wind power generation systems
have come a long way in recent years. Whereas windmills used to
be massive and noisy, today very tiny, fairly powerful systems can
be purchased for RVs, which means they are perfectly amazing
little portable power plants. Unfortunately, like the solar power
generation systems, windmills require massive fossil fuel inputs to
manufacture.

Several years ago, when my adult children were teenagers, my
husband and I joked about getting a bike generator to hook up to
the television. We thought of allowing our teens to watch as much
television as they wished, but to do so, they would have to generate their own electricity. As it turns out, it was an empty threat,
but the idea still intrigues me, and I have contemplated, ever since,
getting a small generator that can be either foot or hand pedaled.
What I like most about this particular system is that it encourages
expending energy to get energy, and frankly, with as sedentary as
my life is, I would love to have an excuse to exercise. Want a cup
of tea? Hop on the bike and power up the hot plate. Want to read
e-mail? Crank the generator to power the computer.

All of these amazing modern technologies require fossil fuels
in their manufacture and transport to the stores around the country so that we can buy them, which is the ultimate irony to me,
but at the moment, these are the options we have for alternative
power here in the US. Solar, wind or muscle (human or…how

about hooking up the generator to a treadmill and having Fido help out? Beats a walk in the snow or rain, right?). We have the opportunity to purchase one or more of these systems right now, and if we hope to have electricity for even a little while into an energy-depleted world, we should probably get one now. The problem is that, at some point, parts will wear out. The life expectancy of a PV system is ten years. The photovoltaic cells stop working. Sometimes the batteries used to store the energy need replacing. Any number of things can happen, but when cheap oil is no longer our reality, we will not be able to replace or repair our systems, and we will have to learn to do without.

There are a couple of power generation systems that are a little more, shall we say, *less refined*. During World War II, when electrical power was scarce throughout most of Europe and oil was a luxury very few people could afford, some folks developed an alternative. A very simple machine that runs off the heat from a wood-burning fire can be used as a generator to conduct electricity. Recently, Middlebury College (in Vermont) built a biomass gasification system to provide heat and electricity to their campus. Another example is a wood-gas system that Dave Nichols invented to power his truck. Clunky and large, it does not compare to the sweet little Honda Prius, but it is also all mechanical, for the most part, and any amateur home mechanic who owns a modern car can attest that a car with a non-computerized engine is far easier to maintain than a high-tech one. While both have things that break, the nuts-and-bolts machine will ultimately have a longer lifespan than the capacitor/resistor one.

What makes a biomass gasification generator such an amazing and intuitive solution for most of us is that it creates power by usually burning wood, and especially for those of us in very wooded areas, fuel is plentiful. Plus, it could (and would) be a multi-function machine. I have probably mentioned before that when one lives on a small space the need for things that serve more than one function is pretty high on the list. A biomass gasification generator would provide not only electricity but also heat for warming our homes and for cooking our food.

The other less-techy solution is a methane digester, which is a very simple machine. Biodegradable matter, like kitchen scraps or animal wastes, placed in a tank create an anaerobic reaction that produces methane, a highly flammable gas. Because methane can replace natural gas in any application, a digester could produce fuel for stoves, furnaces, hot water heaters or generators.

Currently, several companies are working in developing countries (specifically, India) to produce methane digesters for home use. These are not yet available in the United States, but YouTube has many videos on very simple methane digesters.

Let's look at some of the pros and cons of the various systems.

| | PRO | CON |
|---|---|---|
| **Solar** | • only needs sunlight to generate power<br>• totally renewable *energy*<br>• completely clean and unpolluting | • prohibitively expensive<br>• short lifespan<br>• not the best choice for colder climates with less sun exposure<br>• in an energy-depleted future, replacement parts may be impossible to find<br>• manufacture of systems requires a great deal of cheap energy input |
| **Wind** | • totally renewable energy<br>• completely clean and unpolluting | • not a good choice in areas with little wind<br>• a system powerful enough to generate the electricity the average suburbanite uses would be expensive<br>• in an energy-depleted world, parts may not be available<br>• manufacture of system requires a great deal of cheap energy |

|  | PRO | CON |
|---|---|---|
| **Muscle Power** | • totally renewable energy<br>• completely clean and unpolluting<br>• good way to get exercise | • for the amount of energy required, system only generates a small amount of power<br>• manufacture of equipment requires a great deal of cheap energy<br>• finding replacements for failed electrical components may be difficult |
| **Methane Digester** | • totally renewable system<br>• encourages recycling wastes<br>• could be the solution for suburban (human) waste disposal | • commercial systems are not yet available in the West<br>• because anaerobic reaction requires heat, system may not work in colder climates during the winter<br>• methane is a highly volatile gas, and it could be dangerous |
| **Biomass gasification** | • totally renewable system<br>• uses materials that are easily accessible in most areas<br>• mechanical components make it easier to build and maintain | • noisy<br>• unattractive and cumbersome<br>• polluting (burning wood) |

My preferred system is the methane digester, because I love the idea of operating my computer using my own poop, but because I live in a cold climate, I know that it is not the best choice for me. A PV system in my climate, where we spend 50 percent of the year under a cloud cover, would not be the best option either. Wind is a good option, and we have looked into it, but currently, the system that would take up the least space, or that we could use on our roof (rather than having it take up valuable yard space), would only generate a fraction of the power we need to operate even the few electrical things we want to keep.

For us, the absolute best option is a wood-fired biomass gasification system, and as long as we keep getting free firewood from the pine trees that do not survive spring and winter storms, we could actually have free electricity.

The best way to deal with a lower-energy world is, simply, to reduce dependence on those things that require electricity, but if like me you have some few things you would like to keep powered up, at least for a while, you should be planning how to do that. Otherwise, in ten days, you are going to feel incredibly powerless, and frankly, that is never a good feeling.

DAY 12

# Waste Disposal

Several years ago, my daughters were working on a scouting badge. One requirement was to think about, discuss and act with regard to garbage. Some interesting conversations cropped up in our scout meeting the day we discussed waste disposal. My husband and I have been rabid...er, *avid*...recyclers for years. In fact, even before we had curbside recycling pickup, we recycled. We saved all of our paper, paperboard, cardboard, select plastic items and cans, and when our recycling containers were full, we would haul it all to the recycling bins in the next town (because they had established a recycling program several years before the other communities in the area — including mine — had one).

So, we were sitting around talking about reducing waste, and I kept harping on the fact that it does not matter what kind of container we buy our stuff in, *as long as it can be recycled*. It took me a long time, and a lot of thought, to understand how wrong I was about that particular idea. Recycling is good, and we should all recycle, and when we are buying things from the store, we should definitely keep in mind the end-of-life requirements for the packaging those items come in. Think about it. If you buy a plastic container of strawberries, what do you do with the plastic container after you have eaten the strawberries?

I finally understood that Reduce, Reuse, Recycle is the order of the three R's, and for a reason. It is good to recycle, and it is good to reuse, but better is to not have it at all. Better is to not require that someone somewhere manufactures this item that we will have to find a way to dispose of. Once I got that, once I understood, the question of what to do with my garbage became easier to answer.

Each week, people around my neighborhood put out their trash cans. We are permitted to have two 50-gallon cans stuffed as full as we can get them. It is kind of like the bulk-rate envelopes at the post office. We have this much space for this many dollars, and as much as you can fit, regardless of weight, is what can be sent — as long as the lid will close, and in the case of garbage, even closing the lid is not required. It just has to be inside the can and not lying on the ground. Many of my neighbors put out two of those 50-gallon trash barrels. Every week.

We also have curbside recycling pickup on the same day. Many neighbors do not recycle. Usually my family has more recycling than garbage, but each week we still have several barrels of stuff that needs to be disposed of.

What would we do if the trucks suddenly stop coming? What if, for some reason, like what the citizens of New York City experienced during those well-publicized garbage strikes, the trucks stopped coming to collect our garbage and recycling each week? My neighbors would have to figure out what to do with that 100 gallons worth of garbage.

I can remember when I was growing up and visiting my grandma's farm in southeastern Kentucky. Back behind the house, up on the hill, there was a cut-out place that was probably a re-sult of a particularly bad rainstorm, or perhaps due to a mine col-lapsing in the area, or maybe it was intentionally dug. The hole was full of the flotsam and jetsam of a disposable life before there were community-wide solutions for disposing of this stuff. I was strongly admonished to stay away from that hole, because what was in there was dangerous. Rusty tin cans, some old metal springs from a bed, rusting barbed wire…lots of items that can cut and scar and cause nasty life-threatening infections, like tetanus.

My grandmother's personal landfill was actually one of the nicer ones, but it was certainly not the only. There were dozens of places like that. In fact, Arlo Guthrie's "Alice's Restaurant" cautions against succumbing to the pressure of illegal dumping, and his is good advice.

So, what do we do with all of the garbage?

The first step is to evaluate our garbage. What exactly are we throwing away? My garbage contains things that are non-compostable and non-recyclable, like the plastic bags our sugar comes in, any plastic containers that do not have a recycling sym-bol, chip bags, empty shaving cream cans, Q-tips, take-out styro-foam containers, a dismembered plastic doll, a plastic spider ring that I picked up off the floor one time too many and decided to just throw away, the plastic packaging that held the nine rolls of 100 percent recycled toilet paper (does anyone else find this ironic?) and other similar items. We throw away one tall kitchen bag per week for our family of five, and that includes all of the gar-bage from bathrooms, my office and the kitchen. None of it can be put into the compost pile, fed to the chickens, burned or recycled. Most of it is plastic.

And all of it could be eliminated by making a few easy changes to our lifestyle choices. For example, we could purchase sugar from the bulk bins at the grocery store. The thin plastic baggies the grocery provides can be reused, and I do reuse them. A better option, however, is to not use the plastic bags at all, but rather to make a cloth bag dedicated to sugar. In our throwaway culture, we think that using cloth bags is such a crazy idea, but the fact is that cloth has been used for centuries, and it is only because plastic is so cheap and so pervasive in our lives that we believe it is a better choice.

Instead of buying potato chips in throwaway bags, I could actually make my own, and I have; they were delicious. Getting away from the mindset that *just this one bag* is okay is the hard part. It is good that my family only throws away one ten-gallon kitchen bag per week, but nothing in there is anything we need to be using or throwing away.

There are reusable alternatives to all of the items on the list. For example, shaving cream used to be a bar that was put into a cup. A special brush was used to wet the bar and create lather, which was used for shaving cream. Going back to this method would eliminate shaving-cream cans. The brushes can be made from all renewable resources like wooden handles holding animal-hair bristles.

We do not have to use throwaway items, and we can make more conscious choices and not throw away so much stuff. The only challenge is making the mental leap from one of consumption to one of conservation.

Of course, some waste we suburbanites make is not related to packaging (well, except for the plastic holding the bulk package of 100 percent recycled toilet paper, for which cloth is a suitable alternative) and is not tossed in the garbage or recycling. In my neighborhood, we all have septic systems. We have a septic tank for all of the wastewater that leaves our house, including everything we flush down the toilet. In a lower-energy world, I will still be able to use my septic system. Even if we lose power. Unfortunately, my septic system depends on an electric pump to take the excess water from the tank to the leach field. In a powering-down scenario, my family would need to make some modifications on how we use our septic system.

First, we would need to disconnect all of the toilets and, instead, use buckets. Most people will ask why, and my response is that modern toilets require huge amounts of water for flushing. In my system (although not all septic systems are like mine), the water goes into the septic tank. When the tank gets too full of water, the water flows into the overflow tank/pumping station. When the overflow tank gets full, the (electric) sump pump empties the water into the leach field. If the sump pump is not working because we do not have electricity, when the tanks get full, the water will take the path of least resistance, which is to flow through the open pipes and back into my house. I have weighed the options: a bucket of poo that we dump into a hole in the ground…water from the septic tank, i.e., raw sewage backing up into my shower… bucket to dump…poopy shower. I have decided that a bucket is a better option.

We would not have just one bucket, though. There would be two: one for liquids and the other for solids. The liquid bucket would be diluted with water and then poured around trees and bushes (not directly on any of the plants we will eat, especially root crops) to add nitrogen to the soil.

The solids bucket would be emptied directly into the septic tank, and the only thing that would be in that bucket would be the waste and some sawdust (to absorb the smell). We can assume that if most other things are going to be hard to find, toilet paper will be, too, and we would be switching to cloth wipes, which would not be thrown into the buckets, but would rather be soaked and washed and reused. With only solids with sawdust going into the septic tank, it would not fill very quickly, and in fact, the sawdust would help the wastes break down. The tank would, likely, never again be full enough to need emptying.

Unfortunately, some suburbanites do not have septic tanks, and in that case, I would strongly recommend acquiring a copy of the book *Humanure*, which explains how to compost human waste safely enough that it can, eventually, be used in the garden.

If one is willing/able to spend the money, composting toilets are fantastic alternatives to buckets. I mean, I will do it, but the idea of dumping the stuff is not really all that appealing. I would get a composting toilet, but since we already have a septic tank, it does not make sense to make things more complicated (and expensive) than they have to be.

Many of our ancestors used outhouses. In fact, both of my parents grew up using an outhouse. It was not until the 1970s that my father's parents had an indoor flush toilet, and I can remember using the outhouse when I was very young—a very scary ordeal for a suburban preschooler. Their outhouse consisted of a shack built over a hole in the ground 25 feet from the house up a slight hill.

Likewise, my mother grew up on a farm and relates stories of the outhouse she used as a child. During the winter, they used chamber pots in the house, and it was one person's job to empty those each morning. I asked her if she would have preferred to use the chamber pot, which had to be emptied (i.e., carried from the house to the outhouse), or just go out to the outhouse, and she said she preferred using the chamber pot.

I considered the idea of building an outhouse on my property, but my father grew up on a five-acre farm, and my mother grew up on a dairy farm with more than 100 acres. Ensuring that their outhouse was not contaminating their food crops was a bit easier than it will be for those of us in the suburbs. Open-pit latrines were phased out for a reason. They are both unpleasant and unsanitary if not properly constructed. We will need to have a better option for disposing of our wastes when flushing the toilet is no longer an option.

After having considered the problem for some time, and after having reviewed several outhouse designs and our current regulations regarding building outhouses, I do not believe an outhouse is the best choice for someone with as little land (land that will need to be cultivated as intensely as possible) as most suburbanites have.

Composting toilets, buckets dumped into an existing septic tank or the recommendations in the *Humanure* book are among the best options.

One more way we could consider getting rid of our waste is to convert it to a fuel for cooking, heating or electricity using a methane digester, as mentioned earlier. Generating methane gas from our poo is the ultimate in self-sufficiency.

For those of us who are dependent on municipal waste systems to take away the stuff we discard, coming up with a plan when these systems are no longer operating is pretty important. There are nine days left. What will be your plan?

DAY 13

# Health Care

Our current healthcare system is unsustainable. Modern doctors are trained to use very high-tech diagnostic equipment, and many are dependent on drugs and fancy machines to treat the symptoms they discover. Without the assistance of these energy-dependent systems, in what is possibly the very near future, our allopathically trained doctors will have a great deal of difficulty treating us.

On a positive note, many of our illnesses are more a symptom of our lifestyles, in particular what we eat, than true disease. The fact is that, without the industrial food machine and with a lower-energy lifestyle in which exercise is a way of life and not just a hobby for the rich and famous, many of our modern illnesses will simply disappear.

The flip side, however, is that many of the illnesses that have been eradicated from our society, like many of the childhood illnesses that most American children are currently vaccinated against, may see a resurgence, and we will need to know what to do about those.

Several years ago when our doctor moved out of state and we had to find a new doctor, I found myself sitting in an exam room with a very young female family practitioner and debating the vaccine question. I told her I was not completely convinced that vaccines were the panacea of modern medicine and wellness. I said that I was not convinced that the merits outweighed the risks and that I did not think there was enough evidence to completely rule out the potential links between the practiced immunization schedule on infants and some serious neurological issues.

She disagreed. And basically, she told me that, if I did not wish to vaccinate my children, I might want to find a doctor who was more experienced with diagnosing childhood illnesses, like mumps and measles. Because most people are vaccinated, she told me, most doctors her age have never seen these illnesses.

I did not change doctors at that time, but I researched these illnesses and found that most of them, while responsible for a great deal of suffering, have a very low fatality rate and are treated with nothing more than rest and fluids. Most are not even treatable with any medicines, including antibiotics. Which made me wonder why the vaccines were created in the first place for illnesses that are awful to experience, but do not even have the fatality rates, even at their worst, of some of our more modern lifestyle related "dis"eases.

In a lower-energy future, we will likely see a resurgence of many of these diseases as vaccinations become more expensive and are not as widely used as they are now. That said, I'm not entirely convinced that the reason we no longer see these diseases is due to the national vaccination program. Vaccines were not even widely used until the mid-20th century, but by that time, the incidence and severity of many of the childhood illnesses against which we are routinely vaccinated had decreased, most likely due to improved sanitation and not due to the availability of the drugs.

Benjamin Franklin wisely observed "an ounce of prevention is worth a pound of cure," but we seem to have forgotten that wisdom, especially when it comes to our health. The best preventative to illness is to have a well-balanced diet, drink lots of fluids (which means clean water, and not soda) and get adequate rest. Being healthy to begin with goes a long way toward keeping disease at bay. Of course, even the healthiest people get sick. Bacterial infections and viruses can not be completely avoided. Germs are an integral part of our environment, and in fact, we need them.

The most effective treatment for nearly all illnesses is adequate sanitation and rest. In a lower-energy society, ensuring that there is clean water will be paramount to good health. This point is stressed on numerous occasions in Hesperian Press's wonderful book *Where There Is No Doctor*, along with the admonishment that drugs are not always the best cure. Medicines, however, have always been part of human existence, and most modern pharmacology is based on ancient knowledge of herbal remedies. Many illnesses can be and should be treated with adequate fluids and lots of rest, but a basic knowledge of some herbal remedies is helpful.

Herbal remedies are used both externally and internally. Used externally, fresh herbs can be rubbed on the affected area, masticated or boiled and cooled and then used as a poultice, or mixed with a medium like beeswax and used as a lotion. Taken internally, herbs are used in several ways:

+ Tincture: usually fresh herbs soaked in distilled alcohol (like gin or vodka). The alcohol draws out the most medicinal value, but tinctures are strong medicine and should be used with great care and understanding of what they do.
+ Infusion: a tea made from either dried or fresh herbs steeped in water. Infusions draw out the most nutritional value from herbs, and are better used as supplements than as medicines,

although sometimes getting the vitamin boost is really the
best remedy.

+ Capsule: dried herbs encased in a glycerin capsule and swal-
lowed like a pill.

+ Smoking: widely used by some of the indigenous tribes in the
northeastern US.

I am most comfortable using herbs in the form of an infusion or
a tea and have brewed many combinations for different ailments.
For example, a migraine/tension headache remedy I have used
combines dried rosemary, dried peppermint and dried chamomile
flowers. The rosemary is a muscle relaxant, peppermint soothes
nausea, and chamomile is a relaxant.

Most of my herbal remedies are made with common culinary
herbs or herbs or weeds that grow on or around my property. If I
had to come up with a herbal medicine cabinet, I would pick herbs
that have multiple uses and would be what I could either grow in
my own garden as perennials (not annuals, because in a worst-case
scenario I might not have access to seeds or seedlings of plants
that are not indigenous to my area) or that grow naturally in the
surrounding area. I would have the following ten herbs in my garden and in my medicine cabinet.

**Comfrey**, which grows in my yard now, is a multi-use plant
and is incredibly beneficial to the homestead. Used as a mulch or a
side dressing, the leaves slowly break down and provide nutrients
to the surrounding plants. My rabbits love comfrey. Medicinally,
comfrey is used to treat cuts, bruises, sprains and broken bones,
and I have actually witnessed the healing powers of comfrey in
an injured finger. Additionally, my midwife recommended that I
steep comfrey leaves in boiling water, soak washcloths in the water
and freeze them. After my daughter was born, I used the frozen
cloths as a compress to heal skin that was torn during the birthing
process.

**Jewel Weed**, a prolific weed that grows in waste areas, is well-known for its use in dermatological applications. In fact, jewel weed is reported to cure poison ivy, and the two are often found growing close together. We steep it, like comfrey, strain the plant out of the water, and then freeze the water in ice-cube trays. We use the ice cubes like a poultice to soothe irritated skin. In the summer, when jewel weed is growing everywhere, we just pick a bit of the plant, crush the leaves and stems and smear the liquid on the affected area, but we use it very sparingly in this way because it can cause some burning and irritation on very sensitive people.

**Lavender** is a fantastic herb to use topically. A drop of lavender essential oil on the forehead, temples or the back of the neck works well for soothing headaches. As an antiseptic, it is good for wound cleaning (and when a nail went through the sole of my daughter's shoe, I had her soak her foot in a tub of warm water containing a few drops of lavender oil) and a good additive to homemade deodorants.

Both comfrey and jewel weed grow in my climate without any interference or help from me, which is the type of plant I will want when things get bad. My climate can be a bit too harsh for lavender, but with some care, it will survive our winters.

My favorite herbal remedies are the ones that also flavor food; my first choice for an incredibly powerful, all-around germ-fighting herb is **garlic**. It is an annual, but if I save one head of garlic, I can plant the cloves in the fall, and by July have a whole 4-by-4-foot bed ready to harvest. I love to cook with and eat garlic, and so we get many of the nutritional benefits of the root, but as cooking kills many of its healing properties, for the best medicine, garlic should be used raw. Garlic is an anti-fungal, and I have used it to clear up an impacted crop in one of my laying hens (we used the remedy and later, after doing some research, found that the most common cause of her particular condition was a fungus in the crop). I have also used warm garlic oil to treat earaches in my children with a great deal of success. They do not get very many earaches, and none of the three youngest have ever had to take antibiotics when they have.

**Dill**, my children's favorite ingredient in pickles, is an anti-flatulent and an anti-spasmodic, and it has calmative properties, which makes it useful for treating things like colic, menstrual cramping and insomnia. It is a self-seeding annual, which means there is volunteer dill every year in my garden.

**Peppermint** works well for easing nausea, but it does more than just act like Pepto-Bismol. It is an antispasmotic and an anti-microbiotic, has been used to treat intestinal illnesses and is a pain reliever. Mint can be invasive and seems to grow well anywhere, which is okay with me, because with so many great uses, I can not seem to harvest enough to last me until the spring.

**Sage** is my favorite herb next to garlic. I use it in cooking meat, and like most herbs I use regularly, I can not seem to harvest enough of it. Medicinally, sage has been used to treat upper-respiratory symptoms, and most significantly, sage was historically used to treat the measles. It should not be used every day or in large quantities, but a couple of teaspoons to flavor some meat, or a cup of sage tea to sooth a sore throat, will definitely do more good than harm. As a multi-use plant, sage also works as an insect repellant, and as a companion plant, it could prove incredibly useful in the garden. Sage is a perennial in my environment, and I have several plants growing in my herb gardens. It should be noted that Native Americans value sage for its spiritual properties, too, often using it for ceremonial purposes.

**Thyme**, a culinary favorite in Italian dishes, serves double duty as another amazing medicinal herb. Historically, it was used to treat both intestinal and respiratory illnesses, but it is also valuable as an anti-parasitic for lice, scabies and crabs. Thyme is a beautiful perennial in my garden.

**Chives** and **onions** are great for flavoring. I often cook with onions, and there is no better accompaniment to sour cream on a baked potato than chives. Both belong to the allium family, which have been used historically to treat high blood pressure. Because my husband's family has a history of blood pressure and cholesterol issues, onions and chives are a big part of our diet and will always have a place in our medicine chest.

My garden would not be complete, however, without the aromatic and flavorful **tarragon**. When I first planted tarragon, it was because I like the licorice-like aroma, and the first time I used it in a recipe, I was hooked. Tarragon is my favorite herb in quiche, and I use it instead of basil in my salad dressings. Like most culinary herbs, however, tarragon is a valuable medicinal as well. When chewed raw, it is good for easing toothaches, because of its anesthetic qualities, but it is also useful for getting rid of intestinal worms in children.

While other herbs might be better choices than the ones I have available (for example, cloves are a much better toothache remedy than tarragon), if they do not grow in Maine, they will not be very useful to me. Some herbs that grow well for me may not grow well for others, and the best advice is to invest in a good herbal remedy book. My favorite is Andrew Chevallier's *The Encyclopedia of Medicinal Plants*, a great resource for finding specific herbs to treat specific illnesses.

As always, though, heeding Benjamin Franklin's advice is the best remedy, and herbs like echinacea, goldenseal, white pine and rose hips are useful as immunity boosters. It is far better to stay healthy in the first place than to have a fully stocked medicine cabinet.

What is funny, however, is that we often spend a lot of time worrying about our physical health and taking all sorts of precautions, from obsessive handwashing to a cabinet full of vitamin supplements, but we ignore the most simple and basic hygiene step that we can take to prevent some rather serious illnesses down the road, and that is taking care of the health of our mouth.

Studies have shown a link between increased risk of heart disease and poor dental hygiene. Periodontal disease can provide a conduit for mouth bacteria to enter the blood stream, which has been implicated in an increase in cardiovascular disease. The unfortunate fact is that a healthy mouth does not have to cost anything, and some very simple and easily obtainable remedies can prevent some more serious dental issues.

Brushing and flossing go a long way in preventative care. Fluoridated toothpaste does not have to be part of the routine. My father grew up without a toothbrush or toothpaste. He and his siblings would chew a piece of wood they had whittled to clean their teeth, and instead of toothpaste, they used baking soda. His family was too poor to afford visits to the dentist, but despite his lack of early professional intervention, my father did not have his first cavity until he was twenty-one. In addition, well into his senior years, he still has all of his teeth, including his wisdom teeth, uncapped and no dentures or bridges (it should be noted, however, that my father did not eat very many sugary snacks or drink sodas until he reached adulthood—right about the same time that he got his first cavity, in fact).

I am a big fan of my biannual visits to the dental hygienist, mostly because I like to hear that I am doing a good job of keeping my teeth clean—it satisfies my need for external validation, but I am too much aware that being able to afford such a luxury may not be part of my future.

Indeed, plastic toothbrushes and minty-flavored, fluoridated toothpastes may be hard to find at best and cost-prohibitive at worst. As such, we will need some alternatives. A very simple homemade toothpaste powder recipe uses three parts baking soda to one part salt (adjusted to personal taste). A drop of peppermint oil can be added. To make this a paste, add about 4 teaspoons of glycerin to each half cup of powder — depending on how pasty you like it. Experimentation may be necessary to reach the desired consistency. Some recipes add a bit of sweetener (stevia would be the best choice).

If I could be certain that glycerin and baking soda would always be available, I would be happy to stop there, but I am not so confident, and from what I have been able to glean, making my own baking soda would be incredibly difficult, bordering on impossible. The one thing I do have access to, though, is salt. Using an evaporation method, I could get salt (in very small quantities to be sure) from the ocean water near my house, although salt is one of those items that has, for centuries, been traded, and it is unlikely that it will simply disappear. For dental health purposes, a salt-water rinse kills bacteria, and used daily encourages a healthy mouth.

Another amazing and readily available, dental hygiene product is vinegar. Used half-strength as a gargle, it will kill most harmful bacteria in the mouth. In addition, vinegar will dissolve deposits of calculus, especially if used weekly when brushing.

Many years ago, in my job as a transcriptionist, the doctor who was dictating said that his patient had walked into his office, held out her hands pleadingly and said, "I am placing my health in your hands." Essentially, she was telling him that he was in control and that he needed to fix her. It is all too familiar a scenario in this country where we are willing to take great, unnecessary and thoughtless risks with our health, because we know that, in the end, our miraculous medical advances will save us. We can smoke a pack a day, and when our lungs are blackened from years of abuse, they can give us new lungs. It happens with enough frequency that even the doctors who perform these miracles begin to believe that there is nothing they can not do and no one who can not be saved, if given the time and the tools.

Unfortunately, we are heading fast into a world where medical miracles mean that the patient does not bleed to death or die from infection when he accidentally cuts off his finger. In a lower-energy future, reattaching severed limbs will no longer be possible like it is today. The average Joe will not have access to a large ultra-modern hospital, will likely see a doctor only in the case of a real emergency and will never see a dentist. There may be a village or community midwife who is also a herbalist, but most people will rely on home remedies, and those people who have prepared by learning some basic medicinal uses for everyday herbs and who practice preventative care will be the ones who live the most pain-free lives.

There are eight days left, and planting that herb garden can not happen too soon.

## How to Make a Tincture

*The difference between using herbs in a tincture and using herbs as a tea are very important. Many herbs have both nutritional value and medicinal value. Making the herb into a tincture extracts the most medicinal of properties from the herb, while using the herb as a tea accesses the more nutritional parts of the herb. For example, nutritionally, rosemary contains flavonoids that have been associated with cancer-fighting properties (like those found in blueberries), but it is also used medicinally to reduce and relieve stress.*

*To make a tincture:*

1. *Finely chop herb.*
2. *Fill a pint jar about 1/3 full of the desired herb.*
3. *Fill the rest of the jar with 100-proof alcohol; vodka or rum are recommended. Lower-proof alcohols do not work well, and higher-proof alcohols could cause kidney or liver damage.*
4. *Cover the jar and allow to rest in a cool, dark place for six weeks.*
5. *Strain herb from the alcohol through a cheesecloth or paper filter.*
6. *Store the tincture in a dark-colored glass bottle.*

*To use, some people will add a drop or two to a tea. Others place a drop under the tongue. Care should be taken with using tinctures, because they are medicine, and many are just as potent as some synthetic drugs that require a prescription. Keep in mind that most synthetic drugs were originally derived from plants.*

*I strongly recommend a book on herbal medicine. An-drew Chevalier's* The Encyclopedia of Medicinal Plants, *a great resource that has both a general index and an index of herbs by ailment.*

# DAY 14

## Cleanliness

I love to hear the stories of my father's childhood. He lived in a four-room house with his many siblings. They had an old coal-burning stove for heating and cooking, and the outhouse up the hill was their toilet. My grandmother's house was the epitome of orderliness. Everything had a place, and it was kept there. There was very little clutter. Messes were cleaned up immediately. My grandmother kept a rag draped over the edge of the garbage can for cleaning up spills on the floor. She kept another rag tucked into her apron string or housecoat pocket for cleaning up spills on the counter or wiping her hands.

Dishes were washed immediately after a meal was finished, and I actually remember my grandmother having to heat the water on the stove (an electric stove by this time). They had water on tap inside the house, but it was just cold water. When I was very young, she still did not have a water heater. Granny had this beat-up, old metal wash basin, a very large metal bowl that she would fill with soapy water. She washed the dishes, putting the soapy plates and

157

bowls and spoons into the sink, and when she finished washing everything, she would fill the basin with hot, clean water, and rinse the dishes.

She used the same basin to wash her hair, and even after they installed an honest-to-goodness bathroom, complete with a flush toilet, a real bathtub/shower enclosure and a hot water heater (conveniently installed in the bathroom next to the shower enclosure), she continued to wash her hair in her usual manner, in the tub on the front porch.

I loved watching her and was fascinated by the whole process. My grandmother was a very quiet and private woman. She always appeared in public, which was anywhere anyone could see her, completely dressed with her hair twisted neatly in a bun at the nape of her neck. She was always dressed in the mornings when I saw her, no matter how early, and I do not recall ever seeing her in night clothes, even though she slept on the sleigh bed in the front room, sometimes where I was sleeping, too. She had false teeth, but I never saw her without them in her mouth. She kept her long, pepper-colored hair woven in a tight bun at the nape of her neck, and the only time I ever saw it down was when she was washing it, which made those days a special treat for me.

First, she would fill the tub with warm water and bring it out to the front porch, where she had already left her shampoo, a towel and a hairbrush. Then, she would carefully remove the bobby pins holding her hair secure, and unroll it, like a length of rope. She would slowly brush her hair to get out all of the tangles, and after draping her shoulders with a towel to protect her dress, she would lean over the tub and wet her hair, using a plastic cup to be sure she wet the tops and sides thoroughly. Pouring a frugal amount of shampoo into her palm, she gingerly soaped her hair, careful not to splatter the soap onto the porch floor or her clothes. She worked slowly, almost with a machinist-like precision. It was an unhurried chore, and watching her, I could almost see pleasure in just this very simple act of washing her hair. After she rinsed out the soap, towel-dried and brushed her hair and fastened it back into a bun, she would toss the wash water into the garden to feed her flowers. She was like that with most things. Very little was wasted, and everything that could be reused was.

I never wondered until years later, why she continued her practice of washing her hair on the front porch using only a small tub of water, but now that I am much older, and I am beginning to think about how our lives might be moving back to the life my grandmother had as a young mother, I am starting to remember the things she did, and I am better able to analyze the wisdom behind her choices.

If one is having to heat water for all cleaning functions, one will learn to be very frugal with that water. It is a very different thing to turn on the hot water tap and fill up a bathtub for a good soak, than to put a pan of water on the woodstove to heat up, and then have to carry that hot water into a bathing area. Water is heavy, and hot water seems much heavier than cold water.

Unfortunately, we are very likely headed toward a life much like my grandmother had, but most of us have never had the opportunity to witness first-hand the solutions they imagined for themselves. My grandmother wanted clean hair, and so she washed it in a tub of water on the front porch. Why the front porch? Because if she spilled water outside while she was washing her hair, there would be no need to clean it up. It makes perfect sense. She was a smart lady.

Of course, I do not have a front porch, although I could probably set up a hair-washing station using my picnic table, and while I might use the excuse that my neighbors would give me a crooked eye as to why I would wash my hair outside, the reality is that I do not really care if my neighbors look at me sideways while I am washing my hair in a tub, and frankly, I will likely not be the only one out there washing her hair. The problem is that, unlike my grandmother, who lived deep in the hills of southeastern Kentucky Appalachian country, we have a pretty short warm season. I could wash my hair outside for about a third of the year without it being too cold for comfort.

My guess is that it being too cold to bathe is why Medieval Europeans were reportedly the unwashed masses. Now that I know what it feels like to be clean, every day, I would not enjoy being unwashed for very long. After a day without a bath, I start to feel itchy, which I know is more psychological that physiological, but it is there, and I can not ignore it. I also know that most shower-every-day suburbanites share this feeling with me.

So, what do we do if the water on tap stops flowing and our fossil-fuel dependent water-heaters stop making that worth-its-weight-in-gold liquid luxury that is hot water? During one power outage here in the frozen northeast, I came up with a solution that worked, at least in the short term.

I have several very large, run-of-the-mill stainless steel cooking pots, which are mostly used for canning. I filled the largest of these with water and put it on the woodstove, where it served several purposes. First, it gave me hot water for washing—and not just my body, but also things like dishes. Second, it provided moisture to our very dry indoor winter air. It was not a difficult or time-consuming task, required very little monitoring from me, and, as with our standard water heaters that operate without any intervention or even conscious thought (except when they stop working properly), I did not really have to think about it for most of the day, except to occasionally check that the water level was not too low. It was easy.

I also have a very large washtub that I bought at a local feed store. It says it holds 16 gallons, and anyone who has seen those old movies where the kids are taking their Saturday baths in a washtub can visualize it. I put the washtub in our shower enclosure then dumped in the whole pan of heated water and closed the shower door. We did not lose our tap water during this power outage, although we did lose our hot water (we have an electric igniter on our tankless propane water heater), and so because the pan of heated water was a bit too hot to step into, I added water from the tap to bring it down to a comfortable bathing temperature. With the shower door closed, the hot water created a very nice steambath effect, making it nice and warm, and because I was in the shower, it did not matter if I splashed and made a mess.

I recognize, however, that many suburbanites do not have a woodstove. The first option would, of course, be to start a fire outside and heat the water there, which would take a little longer than on my woodstove and would require much more attention than I must give my pan of water, but it would work.

Another option is to build a fire, but instead of heating a pan of water (which then, has to be carried back into the house while steaming hot), add non-porous rocks. Heat these, and then, after a tub has been filled with water, add the hot rocks to the tub. Small amounts of water boil surprisingly fast using only the hot-rock method, and it would not take too many rocks to get a tub of water up to a comfortable temperature for bathing. The benefit of using this method rather than boiling the water outside and bringing it in is that hot rocks, while just as dangerous as hot water for the burn potential, are lighter and easier to transport than a pan of unsteady hot water.

The concerns about using this method include the potential for rocks to explode and cause injury or damage from flying rock shards. However, selecting the right rock will eliminate this issue. When choosing rocks, be sure not to take rocks that are near a water source, including dry creek beds, and to make sure that the rock is actually a rock and not a piece of brick or concrete. Another concern is that hot rocks dropped into a plastic tub of cold water might damage the tub, but this hot-rock method of heating liquids has been used by Natives to boil sap in birch bark containers, and so the risk of damaging even the common plastic tubs in most suburban homes with hot rocks is minimal.

Of course, we Americans are most interested in ease and convenience, which have been the hallmarks of our existence. Nearly every task is accomplished with the flick of a switch, and the need to take extra time and extra energy for bathing may result in us becoming the next great unwashed masses.

If I had unlimited resources, I would make some big changes to my bathing infrastructure. My ideal choice would be to install a Japanese-style bath in place of the current American-style bathtub I have right now. In the interest of full disclosure, I have a Jacuzzi-style tub, which is very large and which I like a lot, but I have what I think are good reasons for wanting to change it.

The Japanese-style tub is much deeper and narrower than my current Jacuzzi-style tub. Picture a really big barrel, and you can get an idea of what the Japanese-style tub I am envisioning would look like. In my perfect bathroom, the water for the tub would actually be heated right in the tub with a wood-burner installed under the bath itself. A few hours before taking a bath, I would light the fire, get it to blazing and then let it go out. In a tub that large, the water would hold its heat for a long time. The extra benefit to using this system is that it would provide a heat source in part of my house that currently has none.

My perfect bathroom would include a drainage system that would divert the bathwater to my toilets (for flushing, assuming we still used the flush toilets and not a composting system) and/or to my clothes washing facilities. In this way, we would be recycling and reusing this valuable resource. The average Japanese-style tub uses 65 gallons of water. The average American washing machine uses 40 gallons per load. I could wash a load and a half for each bath we took and use half the water we use now.

In America, most of us are unfamiliar with the Japanese-style of bathing, and I know that readers will be thinking about all of the dirt and soap in the bathwater. A Japanese bath is not used for "cleaning" as much as it is for "cleansing." In short, there is no soap in the Japanese bath, which is another reason having the fire in the bathroom area would be beneficial. In a Japanese-style bath, the bather first washes in an area outside of the tub. Picture my grandmother with her tub of water out on the porch. Now imagine standing in a tiled area with a floor drain and a bucket or pan of water, which is used to wash and rinse. Once clean and rinsed, the tub is used only for a soaking. I have read that the bathing ritual is a family affair, and everyone enjoys the bath at the end of the day, together.

I was talking with a friend one day about my Japanese bathtub idea, and she said, if she had the money, she would build a sauna or a steam bath. This friend had spent time in places like Russia and Finland where steam baths are part of the culture. Many cultures use the combination of moist heat and cold water as a cleansing tool, and the idea is quite intriguing to me. Having enjoyed a sauna after a swim at the health club, I could see how it would be invigorating, and knowing how the body works, I understand that, without the use of harsh chemical cleansers, antiperspirants and deodorants, the average person does not really have a foul odor as long as he is clean. Sitting in a steam room and then sponging off with cold water is enough to clean most people.

My small piece of land would not support building a sauna outside, and I do not have a lot of space for one inside either, but there are other options for something similar. The most simple, of course, is a sweat tent or sweat lodge. Sweat lodges can be used in most environments, including in the snowy Northeast, but running from the lodge to the house would certainly require some acclimation, and maybe a pair of sturdy shoes.

A sweat tent, like those constructed by Native Americans, is most often used for purifying, rather than cleansing, but it does have the same effect as a sauna. A very simple sweat tent can be built using saplings interwoven into a low structure (not more than four feet tall at its highest curve). The idea is to keep it small so that more heat is retained. We built a large lodge, not a sweat lodge, but it can give you an idea of what it looks like.

Brace saplings are driven into the ground at an angle away from what will be the center of the structure. Saplings on opposites are carefully bent and brought to the center and then twisted together. Once the brace pieces are in place, the support pieces are woven through the foundation pieces. No nails or glue or straps are usually needed, except where the end piece of a sapling is too short to

reach the next brace piece or where the ends of the sapling are too thick to be very flexible. It is an incredibly strong structure, and this model was actually used for housing in some Native tribes. For use as a sweat lodge, it would have to be much smaller than the one shown in the picture.

Using a tarp, insulative blankets, animal skins or evergreen boughs, cover the entire frame. A small pit dug in the center holds rocks that are heated on a fire outside the lodge; to produce the desired steam, water is poured over the hot rocks. Please note that the fire is not built inside the sweat lodge.

In *Where There Is No Doctor*, the authors continually drive home the point that cleanliness is the first, and best, defense against disease, and while we Americans may be a little too sanitized, when life gets a little harder for us and water and soap are not as readily available, it is not too difficult to imagine us slipping off the edge into the other extreme. It was not so very long ago that doctors went from the morgue to the operating room without washing their hands. Until recent years, the number one killer of children under the age of five was diarrhea, a condition (not a disease) that is almost completely preventable with basic sanitation practices.

In the PBS programs *Frontier House* and *Colonial House*, the producers set up a scenario in which participants attempted to re-create what life was like for settlers in the Old West and in the New World, respectively. Both groups seemed to agree on one thing: how much cleaner we are today than people were back then, and I submit that giving up our overly sanitized lives might be worthwhile, but we should fight, tooth and nail, to keep our standards of cleanliness. I know that sounds contradictory, but what I mean is that we can give up the notion that we all need to smell like roses and have squeaky clean hair, but not give up the knowledge of the benefits of good sanitation.

What I noticed in the PBS series were the participants' hands, which always seemed so dirty, especially around the fingernails. Living as I do, there are many (too many) opportunities for me to get dirt under my nails. I am pretty anal about some things, and clean hands probably top the list, because I am the one who does most of the cooking. Obviously, I use the tap with the always-available clear running water to clean my hands, but if I did not have that option, I would need to think of something else.

Our ancestors were incredibly resourceful people, and if we look to history for some solutions, we will find some great inventions to help us in our future. One is the wash pitcher and bowl. My husband's uncle is a collector of antiques, and he has this amazing old washstand complete with a porcelain bowl and matching wash pitcher. It is a gorgeous piece of furniture, and while I am not advocating the purchase of expensive antiques, the idea is one we should consider for our future. A bowl with clean water and a dash of chlorine bleach is a great quick and easy hand sanitizer.

Keeping ourselves clean is great, but we also need to consider how we will keep our homes clean. The phrase, "keep it simple, silly" or KISS is a good one to remember when it comes to home cleanliness; the most basic tools and the most simple cleaners are actually the best. A broom, a rag mop, a good stiff scrub brush, vinegar, bleach and baking soda will take care of most cleaning tasks.

The biggest problem we suburbanites will have with home cleanliness will be the wall-to-wall carpeting that is so prevalent in our homes. When I was six, my father was stationed in Germany. We had lived overseas for several years, and he had received his orders to move back to the States. My mother was shopping for gifts to bring back to family members, and she was stumped with regard to what she could purchase for my grandmother, who had very simple tastes and generally made most of the things she needed. She made all of her own clothes, using one pattern for all of her dresses, but because they were all different fabrics, colors and textures, it took me years to realize it was the same design. Buying clothes for her was not an option. She was incredibly frugal and reused just about everything, but she also did not have a huge amount of space to store things that were not used regularly, like knickknacks. A lovely china cabinet held the everyday dishes, and a gorgeous maple buffet stored the everyday silverware. Granny's house was efficiency in action, and there just was not space for things that did not serve a useful, everyday function.

My mother was stumped. We were standing in front of a display of gorgeous, ornate wool rugs, and so I suggested getting her a rug. My mother, frustrated at her lack of ability to find the perfect gift for her mother-in-law, told me that Granny did not have a vacuum cleaner to clean the carpet. My suggestion to buy her one of those also was immediately nixed, and I said she could use a broom. I really thought we should get her a rug, because I remembered that the floors were a cold, hard and not terribly pretty linoleum.

Of course, my mother did not buy a rug, as it would have been something my grandmother could not use and would have had a hard time keeping clean. Years later, and now that I have my own house with wall-to-wall carpeting in most rooms like every suburbanite, I have come to appreciate the insight my mother had in not forcing such a time-consuming floor covering on my grandmother. The rug would have remained beautiful for about four months, but living like she did on a subsistence farm, it would have been sullied far too quickly, and the lovely gift would not have lasted long enough for my grandmother to really appreciate it. Or worse, she would have simply rolled it up and stored it in the closet or somewhere out of the way so that it would not get dirty when one of my uncles, or one of us grandchildren, came into the house from someplace like the barn, with very dirty shoes.

With regard to cleanliness, I, like most suburbanites, now face the same dilemma that my grandmother would have been forced to solve. How will I keep my carpets clean, in a lower-energy future, when a greater portion of our lives will be lived outdoors where it just is not clean? And the answer is that I won't. The carpets have to go. The problem is being able to afford to put down a different floor covering. We might think that the cheapest solution is linoleum, but if we are replacing carpet, because we believe that we are going into long-term crisis mode, in which replacing things that get worn out will be difficult, we probably want to choose something that is more resilient. Linoleum has a lifespan of about 15 years (as do most artificial products), and because it is a petroleum-based product, disposing of it in a lower-energy future might be very difficult.

Employing the KISS solution is probably the best, and the easiest solution to the question of how to cover the subfloor is... don't. Well, do, but not with some semi-permanent floor covering.

My choice, if I had the money to spend on reflooring my whole house, would be to put natural wood (not wood-like laminate flooring) or ceramic tile throughout. Both are long-term flooring options, unlike the more modern carpeting and linoleum options, and both, if cared for, will last longer than the house. Unfortunately, wood flooring is expensive, and so for replacing the carpets, where a traditional floor covering is too expensive, consider a floor cloth. Traditionally a floor cloth was made by rubbing a piece of canvas or denim with linseed oil. After the cloth is dry, a design is then applied using a non-acrylic paint (oil-based paints work well). The cloth will stand up to foot traffic, probably better than carpets will. A 72-inch 100-yard roll of 100 percent cotton floor canvas, depending on where it is purchased, will cost around $400 but will be enough canvas to cover 1,800 square feet of floor space. (allenscanvas.com/100%20yd%20rolls.html)

Another option is simply painting the plywood subfloor. While neither option is as pretty as carpet, the fact is that cleaning a painted plywood floor or a plywood floor overlaid with a floor cloth is infinitely easier and uses a lot less energy than trying to clean a carpet.

Life may become exponentially more difficult in a lower-energy future, but keeping ourselves and our homes clean does not have to be. In fact, keeping clean may be the key to holding onto our humanity, as any war survivor can tell you. The power of a bath can not be overrated, especially when so many of life's little pleasures will be gone.

With only seven days left, remembering that *cleanliness is next to godliness* and treating ourselves like the divine beings that we are should be one of our priorities.

DAY 15

# Tools

*Men have become fools of their tools.*
— HENRY DAVID THOREAU —

There is an ongoing debate between my husband and my son-in-law. It has to do with splitting the growing pile of wood between the road and our fence. Like most people, my son-in-law is still deeply entrenched in the consumer culture, and the best way to accomplish a task is the fastest way possible. He believes we should rent a splitter so that we can take care of the project — just get it over with. My husband's plan is to split it a little at a time, by hand, through the warmer months, and then by the time the snow starts to fly, it will all be split and stacked. It will take him all summer, but it will get done. Sure, he could get it all done in a weekend with a rented splitter, but it is not about getting it done as quickly as possible. It is not about speed and efficiency (although whether a log splitter is actually more "efficient" is open for debate). It is about self-sufficiency, and the use of a gasoline-powered machine, though faster, does not hone the muscles necessary for splitting wood long-term; by building those muscles now, when he does not need them, my husband will be assured that when he has no choice, when it is split wood or freeze and starve (because when it comes to that, we will need the wood for cooking, too), he will be able to rise to the occasion without ache or injury.

While making homemade pizzas one evening, as I patted the dough on the stone, I remarked that the dough was very pliable, and that I did not really need that fancy-smancy pizza dough rolling pin I had bought a few years ago. My husband just nodded, and added that it seemed we discovered that fact a lot — many of the activities for which we think we need some special tool, we discover, in the end, are just as easily accomplished by simply doing the activity by hand. The gas-powered wood-splitter is one example. A rolling pin designed and used specifically for rolling out pizza dough is another. We are often duped into believing that this tool or that will make our lives easier, when in fact, the advice to KISS or "keep it simple, silly" is actually the best.

So, instead of a gas-powered wood splitter, my husband uses a maul and some wedges. The work is more physically demanding, and it takes longer, but it is also infinitely more satisfying, and when he has split all of the wood he wishes to split, he carries the maul into the house and puts it in its place, and he is done for the day. If he had used the wood splitter (which does not require the same physical toll as splitting wood with an ax or a maul, but is fairly physical work, nonetheless), at the end of the day, he still has a half hour's worth of work to clean and put away his tool.

When we had our pizza roller discussion, I quipped that fancy tools did not necessarily make the job easier. Sometimes, they just mean more dishes.

I will admit, however, that some tools are useful. In fact it is the invention of tools that ultimately gave man control over his environment. Suddenly, this weak, hairless, nearly defenseless creature could do things with *things* that other animals could not do. A stone with pieces strategically chipped away made a sharp edge, and attached to a pole, made a spear, which gave man the ability to hunt animals from safer distances. A piece of metal hammered into a curve and attached to some wooden handles and then pulled by a horse could break apart thick sod more easily than a man with a simple shovel. Tools enabled us to become formidable hunters and, eventually, to become farmers. Tools allowed us to take control of and reshape the land to satisfy our needs.

Modern farming requires incredibly high-tech and energy-intensive equipment, but modern farms are also hundreds or thousands of acres, usually planted in a monoculture (like 1,000 acres of corn, for instance). Gasoline-powered tractors do everything from plowing the fields to harvesting the crops, but before machinery, these tasks had to be done either by hand or with the help of draft animals. An acre of land is approximately 40,000 square feet, the amount of land that one man with a horse could plow in one day, but without a horse and a plow, that 40,000 square feet would take much longer to prep for planting, and then would be an all-day project through the entire growing season just to maintain. On 1,000 acres without the help of machinery, much of the crop goes unharvested, or more likely, unplanted.

As such, when it comes to cultivating the land, I think those of us with smaller lots actually have an advantage over those with larger pieces of land because fewer and more simple tools will suffice. Building raised beds, turning the soil and planting the beds requires only the most simple and inexpensive tools: a shovel or two, a small hand spade and a rake.

Over the years, we have had many shovels. The best is one with a half-sized handle made entirely of metal. It's easy to maneuver, even for the kids, because it has a shorter handle, and the metal won't rot (or splinter), which means that it's more durable. While we should all be completely organized, like my grandmother, and have a special place for everything and be sure that everything is always put back in its place, that's not the way things work at my house. So, having a shovel that can survive a winter buried under the snow is good for us. For digging and turning soil, a simple garden shovel works best in small spaces, and nothing fancier is usually needed.

Being in Maine, our tool shed includes snow shovels. Shoveling snow (especially the heavy wet stuff) can be incredibly difficult work. I provide transcription services for a physical therapy clinic, and during the winter, a significant number of their clients are people who have been injured shoveling snow (after not having shoveled snow or used those muscles for anything for a long time). It is to my advantage to do it manually now so that when gasoline is not available or becomes too expensive to waste on snow-removal apparatus, I will already have my body trained to know what to do without risking injury to myself. In a world where we will depend on muscle power, injury is not an option.

Depending on one's location, a snow shovel may not be necessary; in fact, snow shovels may not even be available. That said, a few years ago, my uncle who lives in Cincinnati, e-mailed me about their snowstorm. He said it took days for them to dig out (here it takes hours). The problem was that very few people had snow shovels, and most were resorting to whatever they could find to move the snow, like pots and pans, or cookie sheets. Perhaps with that lesson in mind, it would be useful to have a snow shovel, even if it isn't used every winter.

In addition to our shovels, we also have two rakes. After ten years of buying the plastic rakes with wooden handles…and having to replace them…we finally purchased a leaf rake with metal tines and a metal handle. The handle has rubber grips, too, which makes it very nice to use. At the same time, we bought a heavy-duty bow rake. The head is smaller and more compact than the leaf rake and was purchased, primarily, so that we could rake out the chicken coop, but I've found that it works great in the garden, too, and I use it after I've turned the garden soil so that I can level everything. One side has tines, which remove debris, and the other side is flat, which levels the dirt. It's also useful for turning the soil when we move the broilers. It probably has a whole lot of other uses, and it's quite possible that I'm not even using it in the way that it was intended, but it works well for my needs.

The other valuable gardening tool is my spade, and we have three or four of them lying around the yard. It's nice for digging small holes when succession planting or planting seedlings in an established bed. Again — all metal with a rubber grip.

Because all of my garden beds are raised, there is no hard row to hoe, as there are no rows, and so I have never really found I needed a hoe. For digging and breaking sod, a shovel works just fine, and for leveling everything, my rake is wonderful.

I don't wear gloves while gardening, usually, but the benefits of a good pair of leather work gloves can not be understated. Mine are military issue, plain black, and I don't think they have an equal. I use them especially when doing any cutting and stacking of wood and when working with wire for the chicken coop or potato towers. Everyone should have a pair...or two...including (especially) the kids.

I already mentioned a maul, which is a combination of a sledgehammer and an axe head. We also have a regular axe, several wedges and a couple of hatchets. We have a gas-powered chainsaw, but we also have a bow saw. For managing the small amount of wood we need each year, those tools, sans the chainsaw, would be all we would need. Some might disagree with me regarding the need for a chainsaw, but when practicing good forestry management, the focus would be on thinning dense stands of saplings (so that the stronger trees have room to grow) and on cutting standing deadwood. For our winter heat, we would not necessarily need to worry about cutting big trees for our fires, and a bow saw would suffice.

A manual bow saw is also safe enough for children to use to cut smaller trees. I have seen it done. In the outdoor skills class my family takes, the kids are often handed sharp objects and instructed to cut down trees. These are primarily urban and suburban kids, like my three girls, and they have learned to work together to use the bow saw. The instruction is "nobody pushes, everybody pulls," and using this cooperative method, cutting down a sapling, for a couple of kids, is no big deal. Two adults using the same technique could fell a much larger tree.

There are other basic tools that we will want to have around the house: a hammer (and a couple of pounds of penny nails), a good set of screwdrivers, a couple of wrenches and a hand drill. Those items can accomplish most tasks around the homestead. One other invaluable tool is a (good-quality) staple gun for attaching wire and plastic to the animal enclosures, although with some tacks and a hammer, the same thing can be accomplished. I just like the staple gun's single-handed feature, but if I did not already have one (or two), I would not go out and buy one now in my attempts to simplify and power down.

As with the chainsaw, having a power drill is nice, but if I can only use a finite amount of power each day, the question is do I want to spend it all screwing two boards together? My (more physically demanding) answer is that if it can be done by hand (maybe slower, but at least as well), it should be.

The same holds true for my kitchen tools. I have a food processer, but a knife typically works just as well. I had a bread machine, but kneading the dough is not hard work; it just takes a bit longer. A coffee maker with a programmable timer is impressive, but our French press works very well, and we also have a camp percolator, which, when we can no longer cook on the electric stove, is actually more useful for making coffee over an open fire than even our lovely coffee press (although heating water in the tea kettle can give us both tea and coffee, whereas the percolator only gives us coffee).

As for cookware, if my kitchen is an example of the average suburban home, there is too much of it, and most of it is never used. If I could only keep one pot, the decision would be an easy one. I would keep my cast iron Dutch oven, and the reason is simple. If cooking in a lower-energy world means that I spend more time preparing meals over an open fire, then I will want something that is easy to use in that environment. Lightweight, Teflon-coated cookware would not last a month used over an open flame every day; at very least, the plastic handles would melt off. In addition to being rugged, the Dutch oven is versatile. I could make stews, stir-fries and scrambles, and I could even bake with it. In fact, we picked up a cookbook recently with dozens of campfire recipes, many of which use a Dutch oven.

A good knife is an invaluable tool, as well. When I was younger, I was always fascinated watching my uncles and my grandfather, literally, whittling away their time on the front porch. They would sit out there for hours with a plug of tobacco tucked into a cheek, chatting or just sitting, while a pile of wood shavings grew at their feet. I do not recall that they ever carved anything in particular, and I don't believe that was the point. It was, almost, meditative. At the end of the day, they would just sit, and whittle a piece of wood to nothing. It is possible that their whittling had some purpose I never gleaned from my simple observation. I do not know for certain, and I never asked, assuming that it kept them practiced with handling their knives. Of all of the tools we might need in a lower-energy life, few will be as important as a good-quality, fixed blade, well-sharpened knife, and a way to keep it keen.

My husband, our children and I each have a carbon-steel blade manufactured by the Swedish company Mora. We do not use them nearly as much as we likely will in the future, but we have found dozens of instances when having the knife as a cutting tool was the best option. The most interesting was when we were cutting duct tape to patch my daughter's vinyl guitar case. We could have used scissors, but for whatever reason, duct tape does not want to be cut with scissors. The knife worked great.

We participated in a Knap-In at our local college, which is a conference sponsored jointly by the anthropology and geology departments during which the visitors were treated to exhibits, demonstrations and discussions regarding prehistoric tools and lifestyles. We learned some very basic techniques for making stone tools. We were advised that, while it was a fun skill to have, it really should only be a hobby, because metal tools are much easier to use and actually superior to the stone tools. Having experimented a bit with stone tools, I can not disagree, but I also can not negate the ingenuity and skill of the individuals who discovered how to make tools and weapons from stones. It was through their ingenuity that we have come as far as we have.

In our lower-energy future, we will definitely want some tools, and there are several that I would be unwilling to give up. In a suburban setting with a finite amount of space, we can give up anything that is powered using gasoline (which will be scarcer and prohibitively expensive, and which can not be stored long-term). We can also give up anything that requires electricity. While some of us may have solar energy or other power-generating equipment, that small amount of electricity would be better spent powering more useful appliances, like a freezer. In short, any tools that must be powered by anything other than muscle should just be discarded.

We might be tempted to stockpile all sorts of tools and gadgets, and maybe, at least in the early years of the crisis, having those things might make life a little easier, but the risk is that in having them, we will develop a dependence on things we will not always have or that can not be replaced. Simple hand tools that can be easily repaired and maintained will be the most valuable things we own. A way to turn the soil, a way to gather leaves and such (for mulch, which is very important for soil preservation), a way to cut wood for heat and cooking fuel, some good-quality cookware, and a knife: those things will keep us human and make our lives a lot more comfortable.

A final word: There are tools that, perhaps, we might need, but not often. Chisels, planers, files, a miter saw, a snow shovel if one lives someplace where there isn't much snow, a post-hole digger, to name a few. We might want to have these but either do not have the space to store them (and keep in mind, that when the on-demand delivery system fails, we will need more space for things like, oh, food, and so keeping a huge tool closet might not be possible) or do not have the money to buy them. In this case, I would recommend a community tool share. This is a good opportunity to chat with your neighbors about setting up a system (either an actual dedicated space where the tools are housed for everyone to use, or a list of tools each household is willing to share and a system for requesting it from the owner). I will leave the operational logistics of the tool share to each community, but if we hope to survive in a world where there is not as much, we will need to learn to trust and cooperate with our neighbors. A really good place to start is with learning to share our toys, and there is not a better time to start than today, when we have six days left.

# DAY 16
## Building a Library

*A home without books is a body without soul.*
— Marcus Tullius Cicero —

When I was in college, one of my English professors told the story of when he was a young man, working his way through college, helping to build the railroad system through southeastern Kentucky during his summer breaks. He was always a book-hound, and whenever he was not working, he was reading. One day, on a break, he was sitting in a box car eating his sandwich and reading a book. This young mountain girl, who had been hanging around the work crew, asked, "Why are you always reading?" He told her he enjoyed reading and that it was a good book.

She said, "I don't believe I've ever read a book…'ceptin' the Bible."

He said she paused then and kind of cocked her head sideways to look at him, and then asked, "Is the Bible a book?"

We students of literature laughed, thinking her so naïve, but the fact is that it is actually a very sad story, and one that is too familiar in poverty-stricken areas. When the choice is between buying food and paying for amenities or buying books, no one I know would choose the latter.

Almost no one, that is.

My e-mail signature used to be When I get a little money, I buy books. If any is left, I buy food and clothes (attributed to Erasmus), and I used to joke that if I were going to max out my (fictitious) credit card, it would be at a bookstore.

On our honeymoon, my husband and I spent most of our time exploring as many quaint, independently owned bookstores in the Rockland, Maine area as we could find.

There are books on every flat surface in my house, including the floor. My favorite piece of furniture is shelves. My favorite website (other than my blog) is PaperBackSwap.com. That I am a booklover, a bibliophile, is well-documented. I like to read a book slowly, to read a few paragraphs, and then set it down and savor what I read.

I like to have certain books so that I can refer back to them. Sometimes when I'm reading a book about a particularly intense subject, I will have nightmares about the book. Some books leave a mark after I have left them, and I will think about the stories or the characters—almost as if they are real memories of true events. I know...that sounds a little strange, but anyone who loves books and loves reading has the same affliction.

At my favorite independently owned bookstore, the owner always asks if I have credits, to which I almost always reply, "I don't bring books back. I hoard them!"

Erasmus is also purported to have said: I consider as lovers of books not those who keep their books hidden in their store-chests and never handle them, but those who, by nightly, as well as daily, use, thumb them, batter them, wear them out, who fill out all the margins with annotations of many kinds, and who prefer the marks of a fault they have erased to a neat copy full of faults. [source: en.wikiquote.org/wiki/Erasmus]

And it is that attitude that makes it very difficult for me to enjoy borrowing books from the public library. I do enjoy going to the library, but not to borrow the books (I love to literally lose myself in the stacks and just breath in the book scent) because, as much as I like having books around me, I do not enjoy *giving them back*.

Which is why I have spent the better part of the last three decades of my life building my own home library. At first it was fiction, especially American fiction, because that is what I was studying in college (to earn my BA plus 21 graduate hours in English), but over the past several years, my focus has been more on non-fiction, especially anything to do with self-care and self-sufficiency. At this point, we have quite an extensive library.

In a lower-energy future, I do not think book publishing will die. We will always have books, and even with all of today's wonderful digital readers, there will always be bound paper *books*, because people just like them.

That said, given what I know of our lower-energy past, I do believe that owning a library, like mine, will be for the Gatsbys in our world, and the average Joe, like me, will not have the extra cash to buy books in the quantities I have (hence, Erasmus's first statement, above—books were, at one time, cherished treasures).

Which is why, if we are going to be prepping for a lower-energy future, amassing a library *now* should be considered as important a part of the process as storing food…and firearms…maybe even more important. As a parent and a home-schooler, I know that the single most important academic subject I can teach my children is reading. Once they know how to read, they can do anything. If I had to choose between buying a gun and buying a book, I would buy a book on how to make a gun and ammunition, and then, because books are so much less expensive than guns, I would buy more books on various skills. At some point, the guy who has stored guns and several years' worth of winter wheat will have a bunch of useless guns, and not much else, because all of the things he stored will be used up, but I will still have my books, plus all of the knowledge they contain. One of us will be in better shape than the other.

If I were going to start from square one in building my home library, my first stop would be my public library. No, don't steal their books, for heaven's sake! Several times a year, libraries hold Friends of the Library sales, during which bags and boxes of books can be purchased for only a few dollars. These are typically donated or discontinued books, ones that have been on the library shelves for a long time without being borrowed. They are pulled from the shelves and sent on to a new life, hopefully, in someone's home library.

While really good how-to books are typically in short supply at these sales, there is always a lot of great fiction. My mother loves Friends of the Library sales. She will buy several dollars worth of paperbacks and send them to us. Contemporary fiction abounds

at these sales, and certainly, having a lot of "escapist" literature in a world that is falling apart is wonderful. I would also search for books on lists like the 100 best novels, most of which provide timeless lessons. I have many of the books on both the Board's List and the Reader's List. I highly recommend collecting as many as one can find, cheaply.

For fiction, I would never pay full price. In fact, if I can not find them at the library sales, thrift stores or used bookstores (in order of cost), I look on PaperBackSwap.com (PBS), but I really like to save my credits (because each credit costs me the price of shipping one of my books to another member) on PBS for hard-to-find or out-of-print non-fiction—like Stewart Coffin's *Black Spruce Journals*, which was on my wish list at PBS. I also, occasionally, get books from Freecycle, a great resource for free contemporary fiction. If library building is the goal, then collecting whatever one can get free is well advised.

For many books, I would simply pay full price, because having the book will enhance my life especially in a lower-energy future. I spent almost $30 on Carla Emery's classic, *The Encyclopedia of Country Living*, which I see is now selling for two-thirds what I paid. Martin Crawford's *Creating a Forest Garden* cost me $37 at a discounted rate through my local permaculture group. That sometimes happens, and I do not regret paying more by buying it sooner. As with other prep items, you can buy it now and spend more, or wait to buy it later, when it might be cheaper, and risk not getting it at all. I normally choose to err on the side of caution when it comes to books.

For Samuel Thayer's *The Forager's Harvest* and *Nature's Garden*, I paid full price, and would do so again. We have several wild edibles books specific to our area, but I like that Thayer's books also have recipes. It is one thing to be able to identify and harvest the plants; it is something altogether different to know what to do with them. Since most of us are grocery-store grazers, wild harvesting is something very new, and we need all of the information we can get. It is a really good idea to start finding the books and learning as much as possible now, while the grocery stores are still available.

I also have a lot of books on herbs, especially herbal medicine. My favorite and most consulted is Andrew Chevalier's *The Encyclopedia of Medicinal Plants*. Another that I will likely use in a worst-case scenario is *Where There Is No Doctor*; my husband's lovely aunt found us a free copy at her local recycling center (another place for free books, by the way). I have already read through it, and the book has a lot of good advice and information — most importantly about adequate nutrition, clean water and good sanitary practices, which are the best *health care*. I definitely can not argue with that.

Rounding out my library are dozens of how-to books. We have books on how to raise animals (including bees), brew beer, make cider, grow all sorts of gardens (from four-season to hydroponic), fill a pantry with home-preserved food, bow-hunt, skin animals, tan hides, build stuff (from cabinets to solar homes), blacksmith, teach poetry, write a resume, start a business and just about any other subject you might think of. Go ahead, ask me. I might surprise you.

And then, there are the children's books…*oh, my…overflowing shelves*.…

If I had no books at all and had to pick just five to start with, I would acquire the most comprehensive resources on self-sufficient living I could find. Those listed above are a good start: Carla Emery, for all-around country living ideas and information; *The Forager's Harvest* or *Nature's Garden* for a comprehensive wild edibles book (but in this case, I would also find something specific to my region); Andrew Chevalier's book on herbal medicines; almost anything by Tom Brown, but *Field Guide to Living with the Earth* has been particularly useful; and the preserving book *Stocking Up*. That is where I would start for the non-fiction.

For fiction, I would start with the 100-best lists or with the American Library Association's Most Challenged Books list, because those books are the ones with great stories, impeccable writing and lessons that we need to remember. There should also be a healthy dose of fluff fiction and dime-store novels. For many years, Stephen King was my favorite author, much to my college professor's dismay. I also admit to enjoying some of Jackie Collins' fiction. Some other favorite contemporary writers are Alice Hoffman, Barbara Kingsolver and John Irving. We each have to pick our own escapes, but in a world that is becoming increasingly hostile, reading stories whose only redeeming value is either showing us that our lot in life is not so bad after all or allowing us to imagine how good life could be will be much more important.

Books are invaluable. In today's society, we do not value them like we should, or like people used to value them. In my grandmother's day, most people had only a Bible, if that, and anyone who had more books was rich. Books were a luxury, and in a lower-energy world, may become so again.

I recently read *Eternity Road*, by Jack McDevitt, about a future world with no books. No books. The thought makes my skin crawl. But there is a rumor that a place where books have been preserved exists. The story is about a group of adventurers who risk their lives to find this mythical place.

But after reading the book, I had to consider which books would I save for posterity, which ones would I want to save that would represent my culture to a future world? I have not been able to come up with a list, because I could not get beyond the idea of a world without books. What I do know for me, at this moment, is that as long as I have a little money, I'll buy books, and if any money is left, I'll buy food and clothing. Because I can grow food, and I can make clothes, but books…well, without books so much knowledge is lost…and if the world as we know it is going to end, the biggest tragedy would be the loss of the incredible wealth of information that is contained in our books.

Let's not let that happen. There are five days left to amass a small library. So, what are you waiting for?

**DAY 17**

# Entertainment

I remember it vividly. It was my first week of teaching, and the wizened, old interim principal told me that it was not my job to entertain my students. He was right, of course, but in this age of television, everything is entertainment. If it is not fun, why do it, right?

Of course, the answer is wrong. Some things that are decidedly not fun (like cleaning out the chicken coop—totally...*not*...fun!) just need to be done, because they need to be done. In the mind of my old mentor, school work was one of those things that did not have to be fun, but did have to be done.

That said, life does not have to be all drudgery, and there should be times when we are having fun. In fact, there should be lots of times when we are having fun. Most children and teens (and a good many of the adults I know) will completely agree with me. The problem comes with the fact that few of us really know how to have fun without something electronic to guide us.

Think about it. You have the weekend off from work, and you are going to go out with your wife, girl friend or group of buddies. What are you going to do? When I was a teenager we went to the movies, went roller skating or went to the dance club. Of the three, only one of them is likely to be a pastime in a lower-energy future (roller skating as entertainment may stick around, but it will probably not be a Saturday night date option for very long). If you plan to stay home, a movie on DVD or video or something on television will most likely be the entertainment of choice.

Most of us are ill-equipped to entertain ourselves, which is why television is such a huge part of our lives. More times than I can count, someone has lapsed into a conversation about some television program plot as if it had really happened, instead of having been created by a writer and performed by actors in front of a camera and then electronically broadcast to end up as pixels on a television screen.

I have been guilty of this, too. In fact, I just finished watching the season five DVD of a popular primetime soap opera. The show is currently airing its sixth season to the rest of the world. My husband is not interested in watching the program, but occasionally, I need to share what is happening on the show with him. He really does not care. *It's a television program, Wendy*, he tells me when I lament on this or rant on that.

I grew up watching television, and so, as often happens, when trying to explain a thought or a concept, I will use some scene from a movie or a commercial or a sitcom.

In the 1980s, the movie *The Wiz* came out. In this remake of L. Frank Baum's classic *The Wizard of Oz* set in the inner city, the Wicked Witch was called Evilene, and she ran a sweatshop. When she is defeated by Dorothy (who also has a dog named Toto, and travels through Oz with a scarecrow, a tin man and a cowardly lion), the creatures working in her sweatshop suddenly seem to come alive. They shed their deformed and diseased-looking shells and step out as beautiful, perfect men and women dressed in white. The sweatshop is suddenly washed clean and filled with a bright light, and they blink, as if they've been asleep for centuries, and are only now waking.

When we no longer have television or movies or even every-day unlimited access to computers and the Internet, I wonder if we will be like those people, suddenly blinking in the bright light, like we have been asleep for decades, and only are just now waking.

Accomplishing tasks by hand is very different from depending on electricity for most of our needs. In a lower-energy future, our lives will become much more physical, but there is a very common misconception that more physical work means more time working.

The fact is that subsistence farmers did not work the long hours we often assume they did. The peasant farmer in Medieval Europe worked an average of 19 hours per week — obviously more hours during the summer and less during the winter. In an extreme survival situation, Tom Brown, Jr. relates that after the camp area is set up (i.e., shelter is built and a water source is secured), it takes about three hours per day to procure food, and after that, it is free time.

Without television or movies or the Internet or video games, how will we occupy ourselves when we are not working? In a lower-energy future, if we are not spending 40 hours per week in some office shuffling papers, then we will likely have a great deal of time on our hands, and if the only entertainment we have had up to this point is electronic, we will be at a loss for what to do.

In 2008, we lost power for four days. We probably could have left the house and found some entertainment, but at least in the first few days, many of the area businesses were without power, too, and so, really, there were very few places to go to. As such, we had to figure out ways to entertain ourselves.

My daughters, being home-schoolers, are incredibly creative and innovative, and while they really do enjoy television and computers, they also have very little problem with finding non-energy-dependent ways to have a good time. During the power outage, my husband's nephew, who was not in school because school had been canceled that day, came over to our house. He is very much a product of our television age, and at first I was a little concerned about how to keep him entertained. I need not have worried. I should have realized that my daughters had it under control.

They took out a book on origami and some pieces of special origami paper and made things out of folded paper. When he got tired of doing that, they played checkers. They ran out of time to do all of the things they wanted to do with him, but there is no real shortage of non-energy dependent activities in our house. We have a whole cabinet full of games, including everything from simple Candy Land to word games like Scrabble to strategy games like Risk and Chess (we have no fewer than three chess sets, in fact). We have all sorts and difficulty levels of puzzles. We have beaucoup decks of cards and a whole book on different games that can be played with a standard 52-card deck, and several card games, like Uno, Skip-Bo and Mille Bornes, that use special cards.

At some point, however, games will get boring, too. For little ones who need busy hands, we have tons of craft items, material for sewing and yarn and needles for knitting. Their boredom could be turned into a creative activity, and, in fact, in native cultures, making things pretty (like beadwork on clothes or carving knife handles) was what people did when the work was done.

Of course, sometimes, we just want to be alone and quiet, but also be entertained, so to speak, which is why television is so wonderful. It requires nothing from us except passive observation, and when my husband and I stopped watching television, we started listening to audio books. Unfortunately, we still need electricity to operate the CD player, but there are several that can be charged using the sun. In fact, we have an iPod speaker/AM-FM radio that can be solar charged or charged with a hand crank.

If we lose the option to listen to books, we can still read, and I have already spent a whole day talking about building a library. As I mentioned, having books to help with skill building is incredibly important, but books that serve primarily as entertainment can be invaluable when there are not a lot of other options. We love to read, both independently and aloud, as an integral part of our daily lives. In fact, each of us usually has a book (or two) that we are in the process of reading.

Games, crafts and books are great, but sometimes we will want to entertain bigger groups of people. It may be that I just gave birth to the biggest hams in the world, but my girls love performance arts, and any chance they get to have an audience they will milk for all they are worth. In short, they love putting on shows, in particular dance shows, but most of their programs have dialogue. My daughters will usually write their own plays, including the ones featuring our collection of marionettes, but at some point, they may decide to start putting on other people's plays, and for that, we have a small selection of some classics including the complete works of William Shakespeare, some Sophocles and a few modern playwrights, Samuel Beckett, Arthur Miller, Eugene O'Neill and Tennessee Williams.

In addition to dancing and acting, my daughters are also musicians, and our small collection of musical instruments includes two guitars, a clarinet, a trumpet, a saxophone, a keyboard, a few percussion instruments, a ukulele and a violin. Family concerts are certainly a possibility in our low-energy future and would certainly be entertaining, if not very good.

We already have all of these things in our house, and my guess is that most suburban homes have an assortment of non-electric games, puzzles and books. Many may even have a musical instrument or two. If that is not the case, now is the time to start getting them.

Games are easy. Simple games like checkers can be made using a piece of cardboard with a grid drawn (the standard checkers board is an 8-by-8 grid of alternating dark and light squares) in pencil and different colored pieces of paper for the markers. A more permanent board can be made using a piece of plywood and a permanent marker (or paint) to create the grid. Just about anything can serve as the checkers pieces as long as there are 12 of each color; bottle caps or painted rocks would work pretty well. The only problem with using rocks would be when the piece was kinged, but necessity being the mother of invention, such things would be worked out.

Dozens of games can be made very simply with very few materials, including Nine Men Morris, backgammon, checkers, chess, cribbage and any using a standard deck of cards. It might be useful to find a couple of books on simple games, like the one we have about various card games. We could spend years learning to play all of the games in that book, and never run out. If making games seems too daunting, Goodwill and other thrift stores always have a large selection of games, puzzles and books at very low prices. Now is a good time to start putting some of those things aside.

I occasionally see musical instruments for free on Freecycle. At least once a month, someone is giving away a piano, and sometimes smaller, band instruments are offered. If I had some extra cash (meaning that money we tend to not think of as money, usually spending it on things like our morning latte or the newest DVD), I would start investing in musical instruments and *Learn to Play* books. Many people suggest that we invest in gold or other precious metals, which might be a good idea, but at the same time, without a way to earn more money, all of the gold and silver will only go so far. I often tell my daughters that if they can play an instrument they will never go hungry. Even in the worst of times, people had money to pay the people who entertained them. An investment in a musical instrument may well be an investment in the future. Gold will, eventually, be spent, but being able to play the instrument will never go away.

An acoustic guitar is not terribly expensive. An inexpensive beginner model can be found for around $100. Children-sized guitars are even less costly. In times of dire financial straits, musical instruments will be the first thing that most people take to the pawn shops, many likely selling for not much cash.

I mentioned our iPod speaker, and really, a solar-powered radio or iPod speaker/charger is not a terrible investment. Music can be calming or invigorating. Most of us have grown up singing our favorite lyrics. Even my two-year-old granddaughter has some favorite popular music. Today's iPods can hold almost a day's worth of music, which is a lot of songs. Even if we lost the ability to change the songs, at least as long as the electronics work, there would be that music.

Even if the work we do is more physically taxing than what most of us call "work" today, it is not likely to be terribly time-consuming, and at some point, we are going to need to find ways to occupy our bodies and our minds when our work is done.

But even more than that, we should always take some time for just enjoying life. In their book *The Good Life*, Scott and Helen Nearing describe their lifestyle. Because they were incredibly organized and efficient, their morning chores took up just a few hours. By lunch, even in the busiest seasons, their day's work was done. In the afternoon, they enjoyed time to learn new skills or practice favorite hobbies. Music, specifically playing the violin, was one of the pastimes described in their book.

Regardless of our individual beliefs on the hereafter, one fact holds true: the time between our births and our deaths is short, and we should take time to enjoy life while we can. Otherwise, what is the point? If we lose our humanity, there is really nothing to work for.

Time is growing so very short. We have four days left. It is a good time to start thinking of ways to enjoy the life you have been given.

## Nine Men's Morris

*Nine Men's Morris is a strategy game. The object is to take all of one's opponent's pieces. To do that, players have to get three of their own pieces in a row.*

*The game consists of a board and eighteen markers, nine of each color. The board has three different-sized squares, one inside the other. There are points at each corner and in the middle of each line on the squares. The points on the middle of each square's line is connected with a line to the inside squares.*

*Each player takes turns placing his pieces on the board. If three of the same player's pieces are placed in a row, that player can take one of the other player's pieces. Once all pieces have been placed on the board, players take turn moving the pieces. Pieces can only be moved along connecting lines. When taking a piece, players first take pieces that are not part of a three-grouping.*

*It is a truly ancient strategy game, and the construction of it could not be simpler. The game board pictured is one we purchased, but my daughter's Girl Scout troop made a game board drawn on a piece of plywood with a sharpie marker, and for pieces they colored small empty spools. The materials can be as elaborate or as simple as one wishes; the pieces could be nothing more than acorn caps.*

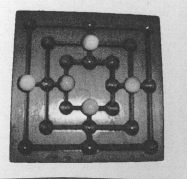

# DAY 18

# Schooling

When it comes to schools, I have long been opposed to the idea that *bigger is better*, and now with the current economic crisis building, the looming threat of Peak Oil and the concerns over catastrophic climate change as part of our daily consciousness, the reality that our schools are ill-equipped for what may well be a difficult future is becoming more clear.

The bigger a thing becomes, the more complicated it becomes to run it, and the more money it costs to keep it going. We do not have to look very far to find complex organisms that require a great deal of energy to sustain. Our culture is fraught with examples, and we have failed to heed the warnings for decades. Instead of drawing down our massive school structures and parsing them into smaller, more manageable units, we have continued to just make them bigger. The problem is that the saying "The bigger they are, the harder they fall" is true, and in the near future, we are going to start witnessing the collapse of our educational institutions. In fact, we are already witnessing this collapse from the overall failure to actually educate our children to the crumbling infrastructures that are becoming increasingly too expensive to maintain and are, more often than not, simply abandoned and a new building is constructed.

The most obvious problem is that the buildings are simply too large. The average number of students per high school is around 900. The average building size for that number of students is 110,000 square feet. The average cost per student for energy/utilities is around $300 per year, or $270,000 to provide electricity, water and heating/cooling for the 110,000 square-foot building that houses 900 kids nine months a year. (Reference source: edfacilities.org/ds/statistics.cfm#)

The sharp, sudden and unexpected rise in oil prices in 2008 caused a great deal of concern to many school systems. Fueling busses to transport students from their homes as far as 20 miles from the school was a concern, but the bigger concern was heating the buildings. At that time, my local school board placed a moratorium on all spending except for essentials, just in case they had to funnel some money into the fuel budget to cover the increased cost of heating oil.

The cost of oil decreased almost as suddenly as it increased, but the damage was already done, and then, in the fall of 2008, just in time for the new school year, the housing market bubble burst and the economy took a nose-dive. Nothing has been the same since.

With plummeting property values resulting in decreased revenue, many communities are floundering. Budgets are being cut to the bone. Services are being discontinued. Public employees are being forced to take unpaid furlough days to save money. Some municipal offices are cutting back to four-day work weeks.

And we have these massive institutions that cost an average of $270,000 per year, just to provide basic services like electricity, heat and water. That does not even include grounds maintenance, snowplowing, meal planning and preparation or staff salaries. That does not include textbook purchases, paper supplies, pens and pencils and crayons. In fact, some school systems have not provided paper supplies or pencils, even to their teachers, for years. In response to rising costs and the need to cut corners wherever possible, one school is changing the font on their printers to use less ink, for a savings of $10,000 per year, which sounds like a lot of money…until one realizes that the savings is negligible, especially when compared to the annual utility bill. Talk about pinching pennies. (Source: news.yahoo.com/s/ap/20100406/ap _on_hi_te/us_tec_money_saving_fonts)

During the Great Depression, there were dozens of stories of school closures due to lack of funds. In *The Worst Hard Times*, Timothy Egan talks about the schools in the panhandle of Texas closing because the communities could no longer afford to keep them open. In some cases, the schools stayed open, without funding, and teachers worked without pay, instead getting the equivalent of an IOU from the community where they were employed. As our communities continue to struggle to pay just for the basic services, we will find it more difficult and less appealing to keep the schools open. The question will be do we want a police force and a fire department or a school? And the problem will be that we can not have both, as many communities learned in the 1930s. Unlike then, we now have these enormous superstructures that cost a small fortune just to heat. In a lower-energy future, we will not be able to afford to maintain them.

Several school systems across the country have already started closing schools. Kansas City, Kansas, Detroit, Michigan, Madison, Wisconsin, Boston, Massachusetts, and that's just the tip of the iceberg for places where they already have closed or are beginning discussions about closing schools. Every municipality across the country is experiencing budget deficits that are affecting the communities' ability to maintain the schools.

Of course, since so much money and time and energy have been invested in these superstructures, we will not easily or willingly give them up. We will continue trying to fund them. Taking history as our example and from what is already happening across the country, here is what we can look forward to in the future with regard to our schools: budget concerns have already prompted schools to start looking at their programs with an eye on reduction. Some schools have already started trying to implement some innovative cost-saving measures, including reducing the number of days per week that students attend school. School-sponsored field trips have been discontinued, and any programs or opportunities that are not already part of the budget are not funded. In my local school system, these actions started in 2007.

Unfortunately, deeper cuts are often required, and the schools must find a way to stay within budget without hurting the students. In situations where budget cuts have already affected school systems, the first things to go have been "extraneous" positions, like office support personnel (secretaries). The next to go are classroom support positions, like educational technicians. In 2008, my local school board and the teachers' union went round and round for months trying to reach a consensus on the school budget. In the end, they were all forced to admit that they could not afford the support staff, and jobs had to be cut.

After that, the cuts start to get a little more difficult. No one wants to do away with the sports programs, and parents do not want to have to pay for their children to play football, and so the bigger team sports (basketball, soccer, baseball) are kept, but the smaller, individual sports (like tennis and golf) go unfunded. Often, the girls' athletic programs are cut to save money.

Next to go are what are considered the extracurricular programming, including vocational/technical training. While having a fairly negative stigma attached to it (the vocational track is often seen as the place for the students who are not smart enough to go to college), this area of education is actually the most useful, and a student could graduate with the skills necessary to begin what could be a fairly well-paid career. Many specialized career paths begin in the vocational schools, including auto mechanics, small engine repairers, plumbers, carpenters and electricians. When we return to a repair-it mindset, those occupations will be the most valuable, and in fact, are already enjoying an increased demand. Unfortunately, when faced with budget shortfalls, these programs will go the way of the dodo. My local school budget for the 2010–2011 year does not allot one penny to vocational/technical training…not…one…penny.

Art classes (like drawing and sculpture) always hold a very precarious position in the public school system, and when cuts happen, they are the first to go. Next is drama, and music falls right behind. After all, the image of the starving artist is powerful in our cultural consciousness, and the idea that one can not earn a living in visual or performance arts, despite much evidence to the contrary, is still perpetuated. The unfortunate fact is that a higher percentage of individuals make a decent living wage in arts-related occupations than in sports-related ones, but when it comes to public money, athletics seem to be more popular to the masses.

The other unfortunate fact is that in cutting arts programs, we are doing our students a huge disservice. According to a study by Stanford University professor Shirley Brice Heath, young people who participate in the arts at least three hours, three days a week for one year are four times more likely to be recognized for academic achievement. We are reducing our students' chances of higher academic achievement by taking away the very programs that will bolster their success. Not to mention that there are students who only stay in school because of the arts education, and cutting those programs will certainly result in an increase in the dropout rates.

General academic programs like math, science and English are never cut, although some more advanced offerings, like English specifically for the college-track students or advanced math like calculus, which only caters to a few students, lose their teachers.

Once the programs have been cut to only offering the basics, or the three Rs (reading, 'riting and 'rithmatic), schools will stop offering services. Like the arts education, special education in our public schools holds a precarious position. When the Federal funding that supports the Title programs ends, schools will stop offering those programs. While they can not deny enrollment to any student, those who need special attention will likely be integrated, at first, into the mainstream classrooms. The results will be disastrous—for the special needs students, their classmates and their teachers. Many of those kids will either be expelled or will simply drop out.

The Federal government also provides funding for the school nutrition program. The National School Lunch Act, passed in 1946, provides commodities to schools so that children, who may not have had access to a regular hot meal, would at least have something to eat each school day. Part of the impetus was likely stories from the 1930s, like the one of the fourth-grade teacher who, concerned about one of her students, instructed her to go home and eat, to which the little girl responded, "I can't. It's my sister's turn to eat today." Unfortunately, our national government is up to its eyeballs in debt, and at some point, they will realize that they have to start making cuts, too. Breakfast will go first, but lunch will not be far behind.

The next step will be to reduce the school day, especially if schools are only offering the basic academic classes. Students do not need six hours per day, five days per week to study English and math.

When none of those things solve the budget shortfalls, the schools will stop providing transportation, and students will have to find a way to make it to the school or be considered truant.

When the schools really get strapped for cash, but they have cut all of the extra fat, they will start dismissing teachers who teach core subjects. All non-tenured teachers of English, science, math and social studies will be handed their pink slips, and the remaining teachers will have larger classes and a heavier workload for the same pay, if they are lucky, but they will probably be working without any other employer-sponsored benefits. The result will be overcrowded conditions in which very little learning is actually taking place. The need for control could, potentially, lead schools back to the corporal punishment model, but I will not go as far as to predict something as dire as that.

In what is likely to be the very near future, our schools will stop offering any classes that are not trivia-based, will not have any services for special needs or exceptional children, will not provide school lunches and will no longer provide transportation. All the while, parents will be responsible for an increasingly higher percentage of the costs of having their children attend our fine, *free* public institutions from rising property taxes to paying for school books and supplies. Parents who can not afford these items will not send their children to school and, unless they have made other arrangements, will be guilty of harboring a truant, which carries a penalty.

Eventually, salaries will be cut, teachers will decide they are not working for no pay, and the buildings will be shuttered.

Our schools are physically unsustainable, which will be what makes them fail. I could spend a great deal of time talking about the poor quality of our public school model, but I will not have to, because it will not be the lack of real learning that will ultimately do the schools in. I will not get into a discussion about the shortfalls of our traditional school model, except to say that, as our schools start to lose funding, their infrastructure will slowly start to deteriorate, as will the quality of the education they provide. In the end, graduates will have no usable skills, because the school model is still based on training citizens to work in the manufacturing industry, which we no longer have, and/or training students to pursue a higher degree, which will become increasingly more unattainable (i.e., too expensive) for the average American.

Currently, 25 percent of Americans hold a bachelor's degree, most of which was funded by government-subsidized student financial aid. Those days of student loans and grants are quickly coming to an end. Already, it is more difficult to get grants and loans, and those who are graduating from college having funded their educations with loans are realizing that they were handed some seriously bad advice. With a national unemployment rate between 8 and 16 percent (depending on the figures one consults), new graduates are finding it difficult to get a job, and if they already have loan debts, they are in a very bad position. In 15 years, the only ones going to college will be the students who have rich parents and the poor kids who have a proven exceptional academic aptitude.

For more information about the poor quality of our school model, I recommend any one of John Taylor Gatto's books and the wonderful essay by renowned writer Ivan Illych, "Deschooling Society," which provides a compelling argument as to why we must, as he puts it, "disestablish school."

I do not disagree with him. In fact, part of the reason my husband and I chose to home-school in the first place was our experiences with the public school system. There were just too many things we did not like, and not enough that we did like. It was our decision to home-school, and as colleges grads, we were fairly certain that we could do as good a job as the public school. What is important to understand, though, is that we did not try to do it all ourselves. We have enlisted family members and community members and hired teachers to help us with our children's educations. We have taken to heart the saying "It takes a village."

Home-schooling, which is a legal option in most states, has become so popular a choice that one family from Germany where home-schooling is still illegal has applied for *educational asylum* to be allowed to immigrate to the US so that they can school their children as they please.

Currently, home-schooling is governed at the state level, with laws varying between states. In some places, home-schooling is very easy, requiring only a letter to the State Department of Education at the beginning of each year and the completion of an evaluative process at the end of the year. In Maine, parents are required to submit a Letter of Intent (LOI) to home-school ten days prior to beginning to home-school their children (usually this coincides with the public school year, and most parents send their LOI in August or September). At the end of each school year, they are required to have their children's academic progress evaluated, usually by a state-certified teacher. Maine's home-schooling laws are pretty relaxed, but other states have more rigid requirements. For example, California law does not currently allow for home-schooling. Parents can choose the home-schooling option by enrolling their children in an approved charter school. In Florida, parents must register their home school as a charter or private school. In Georgia, parents must join an established home-school association.

If the laws governing home-schooling seem confusing and strange, understanding the different home-schooling philosophies is like navigating the Amazon jungle. Some parents choose to purchase a pre-written curriculum that provides daily lessons in the core academic areas and include teacher materials, which the parents can use to teach lessons and grade papers. Some curriculum publishers also offer support from paid professionals. Parents in states where cover schools are required can purchase curriculum materials and list those as their cover school. In home-schooling circles, parents who use curriculums are called the "school-at-home" home-schoolers.

Then, there is the opposite end of the spectrum — the parents who do not use any materials at all. Learning is completely child-centric. That is, the children basically do what they want all day, and learning takes place naturally as a part of life. The philosophy is that children will better learn and retain information about the things that most interest them, and further, that they will find the information they need to pursue their interests. For example, if a child is interested in ship-building, he will find what he needs to know to become a ship-builder. In home-schooling circles, parents who prefer a child-centric style of home-schooling have been dubbed "unschoolers."

There are as many degrees in between the two extremes as there are home-schoolers. Some parents choose a curriculum and follow the portions that make sense, discarding that which does not work for them. Other parents eschew all rote-learning activities, but pursue outside classes and educational opportunities, often organizing classes and hiring teachers (or in some cases, teaching the classes themselves) in subjects that are of interest to their children.

The point is that home-schooling is not a one-size-fits-all; there are many different options and opportunities. The image of the home-schooler sitting at the table doing workbook exercises is not necessarily the norm, nor is it the only choice.

As our schools fail, more parents will turn to home-schooling, but I do not believe that most parents will find the school-at-home model is the one that works best for them. For many it is too rigid, and a lot of parents are concerned that they do not have the necessary education themselves to be the *teacher*. Instead, what is more likely is that small groups of families will form an educational co-op or association for the purpose of supporting each other, academically and socially.

There are several home school co-ops in my area, and they operate differently, depending on the parents in the group, but the basic methods are the same. Parents meet at designated times during the year to discuss academic goals. They decide on classes that they would like their children to take (either from making that decision for the children or from having discussed it with the children). Co-op classes usually meet once a week for several hours a day.

In most co-ops, the parents divide up the teaching duties, and there is no tuition for classes. Fees, if any, go to purchase materials and/or pay for the space used by the group. Most home-school co-ops meet either in a church or at someone's home. Some parents, however, prefer to have someone else do all of the teaching, and in that case, a space for the classes is found and a teacher is hired. This model is similar to the one-room school house, and there are actually some alternative schools that are currently operating on this model. Parents pay a fee for the space and the teacher, who will write and teach lessons on several subjects over a several-hour period one or two days per week. This option can be fairly pricey, however, and many home-schoolers, who are statistically more often single-income families, have a hard time affording the fee-based co-op model.

There are usually very active communities, however, that do not require memberships like co-ops do. Community members will often decide to organize a single class and offer it to the group on a per-class fee structure. In my community, classes run the gamut from outdoor skills/bush craft to biology labs to literature-based writing for teens.

Other community resources for home-schoolers include educational-based non-profit organizations that offer art and music classes. There are also programs like Mad Science. Libraries offer wonderful educational opportunities, like the summer reading programs, and it has been my personal experience as a home-schooler that community members are all too willing to share their expertise with a group of kids. We have been on tours of farms, local restaurants, the local candy-maker, the fire station, the water treatment plant and the grocery distribution center. In addition, most communities have some amazing resources like museums and zoos, walking trails, state parks, nature preserves and, in my area, a huge salt marsh and the beach.

Another great resource for home-schoolers is the local and state government. As citizens of our community, we are more than welcome to attend all public town council meetings, and we can also contact our state representatives for the opportunity to visit the state house.

We rarely have the problem of not enough to do, but rather the opposite of not enough time to explore everything that is available to us. I was a member (and moderator) of a national home-school e-group for a few years, and from what I saw, my community is not an anomaly. The home-school communities nationwide are very active and offer dozens of educational opportunities to their members.

What makes the home-schooling classes so remarkable, though, is not the choices, it is not that the teachers are so much better than public school teachers or that the material they cover is so much more interesting, or even that home-schooled children are necessarily better behaved or more attentive than publicly schooled children (some are, some are not, and it really depends entirely on the kid). What makes home-schooling classes so much more successful than comparable public school classes is (the obvious) that most of the kids want to be there and (the less obvious) that the students are multi-aged, which often reduces the potential for competition and bullying. In a multi-aged classroom, the older kids will naturally want to help and defend the little kids, and the younger kids will naturally want to reach the higher levels of the older children. It becomes a cooperative learning experience instead of a competition between peers. The big kids get to be both teacher and student, and the younger children are challenged by their classmates' more advanced skill level.

In my many years of experience as a home-schooler observing multi-aged classes, the material has rarely been dumbed down for the younger kids. In the typical home-school class, the parents are also there to help the younger kids, and so there is the teacher, who is teaching to the level of the oldest kid, there are the kids, and there are the parents, and everyone is learning. Usually, it is an incredibly positive experience for the whole group.

In our lower-energy future, we will need to scale our schools down, and rather than being completely focused on academic achievement and college preparation, we will need to offer our students a more skills-based education.

The fact is that most of what teachers spend so much time telling students could, just as easily, be learned from independent study, and to waste valuable time trying to force-feed our children this information is doing all of us a disservice. There is no evidence to prove that sequestering children in school buildings with their same-aged peers for eight hours per day, five days a week, 180 days per year while a teacher tells them all about the Boston Tea Party and reads poetry is the only way learning takes place. In fact, there is significant evidence to support that there are numerous ways to present information that have nothing to do with classroom instruction.

Our current school model is a product of the Industrial Revolution that was spurred on by a glut of cheap energy. Cheap energy is a thing of the past, and like many of the things we have taken for granted over the past two centuries, compulsory education will prove as antiquated as a '57 Chevy.

If we are to have any hope of giving our children a future, we need to start now with changing the attitudes from one of making "money" to one of making a "living." We need to change our mindset from the belief that independence is related solely to one's income to the understanding that true independence comes from being able to provide for most of one's own needs. The only way to make that transition will be through education, but not the kind of education that requires children to sit quietly in a room with same-aged peers and an adult teacher who lectures tirelessly.

Whether it is home-school, an educational co-op, a one-room schoolhouse or something completely different that we have yet to develop, our survival in a lower-energy future will depend on our ability to provide our children a skills-based education that will enable them to become self-sufficient, and not on whether they can achieve a high SAT score.

There are three days left, and our success as a species will depend on our ability to adequately educate the future generations.

**DAY 19**

*Networking*

The idea of Transition Towns fascinates me. From my understanding, the idea is to create these communities...and that's kind of where they lose me. The idea of *creating community*. It's so... Orwellian to me.

I do not think communities can be created. Rather, I think they just happen. I have lived all over the United States and in other countries, and what I have discovered is that there is a tendency for *birds of a feather to flock together*. In short, whether we mean to do it or not, whether it is a conscious decision or not, we tend to move into neighborhoods where the other people who live there seem to be like us. In a country that purports to be a melting pot (and in a lot of ways, we are much more integrated than many other countries), more often than not, we tend to segregate ourselves, and whether we mean to or not, our communities are often divided along ethnic and/or racial lines. I think, for the most part, we just either are not aware of it or we just choose to ignore it. Even our planned communities will end up being segregated, whether the founders of these proposals intend it or not. Most of the eco-village proposals are being marketed to young urban professionals and suburbanites. The cost, alone, will prevent most of us from being able to afford to live there.

That said, I have never actively sought to cultivate diversity in my life. I grew up, for the most part, in middle-class neighborhoods around middle-class people with middle-class values. I went to school with a whole lot of people who were very different from me, but, frankly, while we had classes together, for the most part, we tended to stick with groups of kids who were very much like ourselves, not always in the way we looked, per se, but very much in the way we acted and thought, and with those who had similar interests. For example, I was in the band, and so, too, were most of my friends.

I think there is something comforting about being surrounded by people who think and believe and act like we do. In fact, I think, for the most part, we tend to gravitate toward those who are most like ourselves, and I think it happens naturally, even when we are not aware that it is happening. I have had friends in my past who were very different, but we were not very close friends, and we were not friends for very long, because the sad fact is that there has to be a common ground when it comes to developing relationships with people.

When I was in the band, most of my friends were in the band. When I was cheerleading, I spent most of my time around other cheerleaders and athletes. When I was a married college student, all of my friends were other married college students, or their spouses. When I started working, most of my friends were co-workers. When I joined the Army, all of my friends were soldiers. After I moved to Maine and was a full-time stay-at-home mom (SAHM), my very best friends were other full-time SAHMs, but then, I started working from home, and became a WAHM (work-at-home mom), and I no longer had quite as much freedom to hang out with the other moms, because I had a job. Then, our children started getting old enough for school, and they opted for the traditional route, but I decided to home-school. Our lives spun off in different directions, and the common threads that had bound our friendship unraveled. It was not ugly, and we are still friendly. Occasionally, my family is invited to a gathering hosted by one of them, or we invite the group to some social thing we are hosting. If we see them in town or at the farmer's market, we hug and catch up, but we no longer get together weekly, and we do not make a special effort to connect with each other.

I have moved in and out of dozens of communities in my life time, and even as I have transitioned from one to another, I have always, at exactly the moment that I needed it, found the community I was seeking. Human beings are social animals, and finding like-minded people really does come naturally for most of us.

But what if it doesn't? And in a lower-energy future, having a network of people to call on, depend on and share with will be critical to our survival. It has been proven that even with adequate shelter, enough food and plenty of water, if human contact is denied, babies fail to thrive. Love, as hokey as it sounds, is critical to our survival.

One of the biggest complaints I have heard about the suburbs is the lack of community. The problem is that we are all locked up tight in our individual homes. We do not live close enough, like people in apartment buildings, for instance, to know what is happening with our neighbors (even when we would prefer not to know), and there are cases where people in suburban settings have lived in abutting properties for half a decade and never met. It takes two to tango, but it also requires that one lead; in our coming lower-energy future, everyone will need to step outside that comfort zone.

When my husband and I bought our house in 1997, we did not know any of our neighbors. In fact, in the buying of our house, we unwittingly displaced the family who had been renting it with no notice, six days before Christmas. The fault was not ours. Being simply the buyers, we had no relationship with the former owners or their tenants, and it was the responsibility of the former owners to inform their tenants that the house was under contract to be sold with a closing date of December 19. They failed to do so, and the family who was renting the house was told the morning of the closing that they had until 5:00 pm to be out. When I was doing my pre-close inspection of the property, the tenants were trying to pack and move. Their Christmas tree ended up on the front lawn.

We learned a lot after we moved in. For example, we discovered that the former tenant's father, who was renting the house across the road from us, was our new neighbor, and the tenants had been trying to negotiate with the owners to buy the house with an owner-financing contract. In short, they had not intended to move, and the owners of the house simply sold the house out from under them.

With that as our beginning, any hopes of trying to build a meaningful relationship with our immediate neighbors were pretty well out of the question. What made it worse, though, was the fact that, for the former tenants, this was their home, and even after they had moved, they still felt a connection to the property. Their pool was in the backyard until the spring thaw, and they had used the front lawn as a parking space for their dump truck, and thought nothing of using it as a place to turn their big dump truck around. I actually had to ask them not to drive across my lawn anymore. It was, after all, my lawn, even if it had formerly been theirs.

I certainly wasn't making any new friends.

In the spring, the family across the street moved, and over the summer, the owners of the house completed some renovations, repainting the exterior and doing some landscaping. The house stayed empty for several months, but in the meantime, I actually was making the acquaintance of our other neighbors. I took my daughter on a walk down our road and met the neighbor with the flower garden, who gave us some flowers. We met and chatted with our abutting neighbor who lives across the brook. Both were single women in their forties with no children. Our other abutting neighbor introduced himself and his wife to us. They are an elderly couple whose children live out of state.

We tried some gardening that year and had some successes, and then ended up with some rabbits to breed. The elderly couple next door thought us quirky, but safe. The feeling was mutual.

We met the neighbor at the end of the road, whose daughter was a year or so younger than mine. They were renting one half of the duplex, but we learned that he and his girlfriend hoped to buy it.

We had lived in our house for almost two years, when the house across the street was finally sold to a new couple. When they moved in, I baked some muffins and brought it over to them. The next summer, the family living in the duplex at the end of the road purchased the house. We had just been strawberry picking and made some strawberry jam. We had extra. So we put some strawberries and a jar of jam in a basket and took it down to them as a sort of "Congratulations on Buying Your House." Since then, every time a house has bought or sold in my neighborhood, I have made it a point to go and say hello to the new neighbors.

In this way, I believe that I have been building community, but I would not consider ours a community in the way, I think, the Transition Town thinkers are envisioning. We do not have monthly, or even annual, potluck dinners. We do not have a formal neighborhood watch. We do not have a community center where we all have parties. We do not even have a Home Owner's Association. We are just several families who happened to buy a house on the same street, and we do not necessarily have the same philosophies about anything; we are not buddies, but we are a community of sorts.

And here's where I will start splitting hairs. I would not consider my neighborhood a community in the way that the old fraternal organizations were community, but in our way, we do look out for each other. When we all lost power several years ago, my husband and I went down to check on our neighbors and let them know that we still had water (several of our neighbors have wells with electric pumps), and we had the woodstove for heat and cooking, if they needed any of those things. One year around the holidays, I had an over abundance of Amish friendship bread starter, and I baked a mini-loaf of the bread for each of my neighbors and gave them each a starter.

When my son was a teenager, he mowed the lawn for my elderly neighbor next door who had had surgery and could not do it himself. Several years later, the neighbor had a reaction to his medication and had to be transported via ambulance to the hospital, and we went to pick him up and bring him home, because his wife does not drive.

But it goes both ways. When they were cleaning out their basement, my neighbors gave us all of their canning supplies. When another neighbor had trees removed, they gave us the wood, and heating our house is free. This year, the elderly neighbor even gave us a chainsaw he said did not work, but it did, and when we offered it back to him, he scoffed and told us to keep it. When our rabbits had their first litter of kits, one of our neighbors who had experience with rabbits helped us sex them so that they could be separated by gender. When my car would not start, the neighbor down the road brought up his jumper cables and helped me start my car. When we have bad snow storms, our neighbor's son uses his snow blower to clear out the mailboxes so that our mail will get delivered, and he has even cleared a path around our house for us.

If a community is a group of like-minded people with similar interests and needs, then my neighborhood is not a community. Rather, we are more like a net, woven together with different strands, going in different directions, but nevertheless connected. We are a network, and while others are encouraging the creation of communities, I propose that we work on developing a network.

I have introduced my neighborhood network, but that is not the only network I belong to. I also have a network in town, which is actually pretty amazing, considering I live out in the suburbs, do not get downtown very often, do not have kids in school and do not have a job that makes me a visible part of the community. To further confound any efforts I might try to make myself more well-known in my town is the fact that I live in a resort community that is largely seasonal, and even if I were a regular customer, when the stores are open, the proprietors would never know if I am a year-round resident or a tourist. Worse is the fact that most of the businesses are owned by people who live out-of-state for most of the year anyway, and they do not really care if I am a tourist or a townie. What's a girl to do to get some notice around here, right?

My first stop was the library. We got to know the previous Juvenile Services librarian. Knowing we were home-schooling and studying German, she bought books for us on the subject. As a notary public, I am legally entitled to perform wedding ceremonies. When she told me that she was getting married and looking for a notary, I told her I could help out.

After getting married, she left the library, and I made it a point to meet the new Juvenile Services librarian. Over the years, she has been incredibly helpful not just with recommending books for us to read, but also with organizing and teaching classes on library skills for the home-school community. When I was volunteering for a program that provided books to soldiers overseas, I mentioned my efforts to my librarians, and they donated a box of books. Recently, the board of directors at the library was considering adding a new member, and they asked me if I would be interested in serving, because I was someone who had a great deal of interest in conserving our library, especially in light of a declining town budget.

The library is an integral part of my network, and while I do not volunteer or make any special effort to do things for them, I am a loyal patron, my girls very much enjoy the library, and the people who work there know us. It is nice to go where people know your name.

Several years ago, when we were organizing the parents' group in town, the Vista Coordinator who was helping us also happened to be self-employed and owned a transcription business. I was also self-employed as a virtual assistant, and I mentioned to her that if she ever needed any help to let me know. Eventually, she decided she did need help. I worked for her for two years, and then, she decided she was finished being a transcriptionist, and I took over one of her contracts. Several years later, her husband was elected to the local school board, and they needed a transcriptionist to record the minutes of the meeting. He remembered that I did that, and I was hired. I was a self-employed, home-schooler working as the secretary of the local school board. They are a part of my network.

My daughters are very active in their dance school, including the dance competition team. The other parents at the dance school are part of our network, and it is not just about dance. My daughters are not the smallest children at the school, but there are three of them, and we have been taking classes at the school for nine years. A lot of the older dancers and their parents know us, and so when dance clothes are outgrown, my family is often offered these gifts. One of the parents is always on the lookout for things she thinks we can use, and vice versa. She found me some quart canning jars, and I found her some gallon canning jars. She often gives us eggs when her chickens are laying and ours are not, for which we trade a couple of pounds of hamburg. She took us to her wild blueberry patch one year, and we brought her to our wild raspberry patch. Last year, when we picked up our quarter cow, we were given a lot of liver, which we realized we do not really like, but the owner of the dance school does like liver, and so we gave it to her. One day I was talking about the movie *Grease* with one of the competition team parents. She found out that a local school was performing the stage production and invited us to go with her and her family. We have developed these relationships with these people over time. They are part of our network, and we know that we can depend on them, and they on us.

We have a network of home-schooling friends, as well. Over the years, we have shared teaching duties, childcare responsibilities, organizing roles, resources and supplies. The home-school group is very large and very diverse, and we tend to flit in and out of each other's lives, much like the butterflies who visit my flower garden. When the time or activity is right, we find ourselves right back together. Because I am also a certified teacher, I often perform annual portfolio reviews for my fellow home-schoolers. We also take a lot of classes that are taught by other home-schoolers or by non-profit organizations in our area. Those teachers and home-schooling friends are part of our network, which grows just a little bigger each year.

For several years, we have been regular customers at our local farmer's market — so much so, that many of the vendors know our faces, and comment on things we have discussed on previous visits. One particularly cold and rainy day, we were just about the only customers at the farmer's market, an outdoor venue in the parking lot of a local shopping center, where the vendors only have a shade cloth for protection. We were making all of our usual stops when the lady who sells felted knit items stopped my daughter to admire the buckskin pouch she was wearing. The vendor was very interested to learn that my daughter had made the pouch, and she asked my daughter to make a couple for her. Suddenly, we were not just customers, but had been drawn into the fold, as it were.

Another vendor sells goat cheese — the most amazing feta I have ever had, in fact, and a quite lovely herbed soft cheese marinated in olive oil they call a "button." Over the course of the summer, we chatted every Saturday for several minutes. As a result, I found out they had raised a couple of pigs, and they sold us a quarter of one. They have a chicken plucker, which they have said we can use next time we raise meat chickens. And I found out that they live just right up the road from us. Another market vendor saves us strawberries, especially early or late in the season, and another knows we really like peaches and will put aside a bag for us. "Grammy," who makes baked goods and granola, will give the girls fruit leathers when we go and is impressed when they spend their own money. I buy tomatoes by the bushel from another vendor who gives me recipes for making sculptures out of rhubarb leaves. We have created a network with these farmers.

The kind of network we have is not a community that could have been created. It is not a "fraternal" organization. We do not pay membership dues. We all have very different lives and very different interests, but there is that one little thing that we all have in common. What is funny is that I will be talking with one person in my network and mention a person, who I believe is in a totally unrelated part of my network, only to find out that they know each other. For instance, my husband works with a guy whose uncle is the butcher we use.

In a lower-energy future, we are going to need these sorts of very far-reaching and intricate webs of networks, and they can not be forced or created. They have to be real, and they have to be based on common interests and needs. For the most part, my function in most of my network is as a consumer, but at some point, that may change, because I have something more to offer than money. In fact, we have already made small steps in that direction with my daughter's pouch, for example, in my role as the teacher/evaluator for the home-school community, and recently I was able to design a web site for some people who teach one of the classes we attend. In another couple of years, we will be harvesting honey, and maybe instead of buying cheese at the farmer's market, we will barter some honey for some goat cheese...or goat's milk to make our own cheese. Who knows? But since we have already tied that point in our weave, it is there now.

I believe that most people already have at least the beginnings of a network. The only people who may not are people who are brand new to a neighborhood, and those will be the people who will want to know what they can do to start building their network.

To get started, think of a bull's eye. The center is one's home. Start there, and move outward. First to the neighbors. Meet them. Take them some home-baked cookies with a little note saying hello. Next, go to some public places in the community, like the library and get to know the librarians. After that, join a committee or find a volunteer opportunity. If you have a child in school, join the PTA. If your community does not have a farmer's market, but you think they should, try to get one. If you live in a suburban community where there is an incredibly restrictive HOA, get on the board and start to make some changes. Most people have some one thing that they feel very strongly about. Pick that one thing and find a place to volunteer to do it. The key is to be a very visible presence in your community. Say hello, be active and more importantly, be proactive.

The biggest complaint I have heard about suburban life is how isolated everyone is, and while I'm not advocating starting a welcoming committee (although that's not a bad way to meet one's neighbors) or pushing the idea of monthly block parties (although, seriously, would that be so horrible?), I do believe that if we feel isolated, it could be that we have isolated ourselves. John Donne wrote "No man is an island entire of itself. Each is a piece of the continent, a part of the main." If we live in a suburb, we are part of that neighborhood as much or as little as we make ourselves be, and our experience will only be as bad or as good as we make it.

There are two days left, and if you have not started building a network of people who can help you and whom you can help, the time to start is today. Some people may think that it is not their responsibility to make the first move, but really it is. We all have the responsibility to make the first move. So, do it. Bake some cookies. Go meet the neighbors. Then, head over to the library. I hear that librarians like cookies, too.

**DAY 20**

*Security*

TEOTWAWKI fiction is fraught with violence. The cause of the end of the world varies, depending on the author, but the result is always the same. There are the good guys, which are the ones most of us like to identify with. Despite the difficulty of the times, they retain their ethics and morals...their *humanness*.

And then, there are the other guys, the bad guys, what many doomers refer to, half jokingly, as the zombie hordes. These are the lawless, gangbangers whose only goal in life is to take as much of whatever they can get from whoever has it, and they will use as much force as is necessary to achieve their objective. Life means absolutely nothing to them, and they are just as likely to kill their comrade as they are to kill a victim. They are ruled by extreme violence. They are almost always men. Any women in their company are subjugated, usually by force, often kicking and screaming.

The zombie hordes are always modeled after our society's subset. Shaved heads, piercings, multiple tattoos, usually unwashed and wearing dirty and/or unmended clothing. They do not care a great deal about their appearance, and satisfying their various hungers is their only desire. Their vernacular often mirrors our present-day street language. It is important that we understand those literary characters are nothing like us, everyday people. They are thugs, and in film and in literature, when they come to a gruesome end, we cheer. Score one for the good guys!

The reality, however, is that in the face of complete collapse in which transportation becomes a real issue, having the roving bands of ne'er-do-wells descend on our tiny suburban homesteads like so many human locusts is not as likely as we might like to think. That is not to say there will never be trouble. After all, even today, when we are relatively secure and, mostly, at peace (at least within our own borders), there are pockets of violence, but it is rare in suburbia.

In many online doomer circles, the issue of security is the hot topic of the day. In fact, after having a lifetime's worth of stored wheat berries, the most oft-stated recommendation from survivalist doomers is some sort of firearm. Which one to get is also hotly debated. Everyone has his favorite. Well, almost everyone. I do not have a favorite. In fact, my knowledge of firearms is, basically, limited to the one I fired while enlisted in the US Army. At each of my duty stations, I was issued an M16A2. It is a high-powered assault rifle. There are two settings: semi-auto and auto. Auto releases three rounds with one trigger pull. Semi-auto releases one round per trigger pull, but there is no hammer or bolt to pull back after it has been fired, and so as soon as the trigger is pulled, another round is ready to loose. We were issued 30-round magazines.

Because of my familiarity with the M16A2, my personal preference for a weapon would be something similar in a civilian form: the AR-15 or the SKS. The AR-15 is considerably more expensive, which may make some believe it is a better quality, but that is also debatable. Again, everyone has his favorite.

An assault rifle's purpose is for use in armed conflict by soldiers to defend a position or to attack to achieve an initiative. It is combat, and it is accepted that someone will get shot. The military assault rifle is not for the personal protection of the soldier who is carrying it. Rather it is an aggressive weapon meant to be used against another person, who is, more likely than not, shooting back. The weapon is not for personal protection, but the gear the soldier is wearing is. The Kevlar helmet protects the soldier's head from bullets, and bulletproof vests protect vital organs.

It is different with home protection. When we are snug in our homes, we never expect someone might try to break in and do us harm. Even in the worst-case scenarios, in violence ridden places like post-collapse Argentina and post-collapse Russia, everyday assaults were not expected, although there was (and still is in Argentina) a lot of daily violence. Typically, we do not assume (like the soldier in a combat zone who is armed with an assault rifle) that we are going to be attacked, but when we are, it is often very rapid and very violent. There may not be time for us to get our assault rifle ready for our defense. Again, unlike the soldier, we are not likely to be locked and loaded and ready to shoot an assailant at a moment's notice.

A semi-automatic assault rifle is a battle weapon and might not be the best choice for home defense. If one is going to invest in a weapon for self-defense, a smaller hand gun is a better choice. As for which one to get, the best advice I can give is to go to the nearest sporting goods store and heft a few, talk with the guys behind the counter, explain what it is you are looking for, and then, after some field research, make a decision.

In the doomer circles, personal security is the most often discussed reason for having firearms, and while it may be a very important issue, there are some more practical reasons to have a gun in a lower-energy world. For most of us on small suburban lots, raising large animals for food is not going to be possible (unless we live on a golf course and turn the last nine holes into pasture land). We can raise rabbits and chickens and ducks, and even dwarf pigs and goats, but some of us may prefer to use all of our land for crop production and procure our protein in other ways. A good hunting rifle or a shotgun would be incredibly useful, and in a pinch could also be used for self-defense.

Guns are good, as a last resort, but I strongly advocate that a good offense is the best defense. With that in mind, the first thing I would do is to get a dog. In 1992, 191 burglars were questioned, and most stated they were less likely to invade a house with a barking dog. It is not that criminals are afraid of being bitten, although some may well be, but because dogs are noisy and attract attention — something most criminals do not want. In fact, the survey revealed that dogs were greater deterrent than all other crime prevention tactics. (Source: tkdtutor.com/07Defense/Strategy/Home.htm.)

I will talk more about the benefits of dogs later, but having a dog, especially a trained guard dog that lives indoors, where he is not as likely to fall victim to something like poisoning, is a good idea. In fact, our chow-chow has been great for alerting us of problems outside. A few years ago, in the middle of the night, she woke us up, and when we checked outside, there were two dogs in our fenced backyard. They had broken into our rabbit cage and had killed our rabbit. The dogs had done this sort of thing before to other people in the neighborhood, but had never been caught red-handed. This time, because of our dog, they were caught in the act, and as a result, we were able to ensure that nothing else was harmed by those two dogs.

Our chow-chow has also been very protective of me and my children. Whenever a salesman, repairman or delivery man has entered my home, especially when I was alone with the kids, my dog would position herself between me and the visitor, and if he moved toward me, she would growl, very low, or bark at him. I was probably always safe anyway, as none of those service personnel ever intended me any harm, but it was nice to have a slightly menacing-looking dog between me and a potential threat.

The second-best security is the neighbors. I work from home, and a few years ago a client was coming over to my house to do some work with me. I saw him pull onto our road, and so I went to check on my daughter to be sure that she was entertained while I was working. I could not find her, and I started to panic, thinking she had run outside without telling me. So, I ran out of the door and called her name, frantically. My neighbor had also seen the strange car pull onto our road. Instead of parking in my driveway, the client drove past and pulled over to the side of the road just beyond my house. He parked the car and got out, but the neighbor did not see exactly where he had gone. She had only seen enough to know that a strange car had driven down the road and not stopped at my house, or hers. When she heard the panic in my voice calling my daughter's name, she thought…well, she thought something might have happened to my daughter, and that the stranger had something to do with it.

That is what happens when one knows one's neighbors. If I thought something was amiss next door or across the street, I would go find out what was happening, and we have before, when we saw weird cars with shady-looking characters driving down the road. Even in the movies, the bad guys do not want conflict. They want total passivity, total cooperation. They might be willing to take on a nosey neighbor, too, but not the whole neighborhood. If total collapse results in total chaos, we have to be willing to protect ourselves, and the first step is the willingness to stand with and protect our neighbors. There is complete truth in the saying "There is safety in numbers."

There is something to be said, however, about being able to care for oneself, and since I am all about self-sufficiency, I would be remiss if I did not recommend a self-defense course. The idea is empowerment, and there is nothing more empowering than knowing that even in the face of brute strength, one is able to defend oneself. In self-defense classes, the emphasis is on immobilizing the attacker and escaping. Which is why I mention self-defense last, because if one's only weapon is to immobilize the attacker and then run, but the attack happens at home, there is the potential of subsequent attacks by an increasingly frustrated attacker.

Which takes us back to the beginning of today. If our society degenerates to "us versus the zombie hordes," the only defense is deadly force, and if one intends to have a firearm as protection, one needs to be willing to use that firearm in the manner in which it was intended to be used, whether it is a semi-automatic, military-style weapon, a handgun or a hunting rifle, to mete out death.

Having spent a lot of my life just studying people, I have come to realize that people are a lot like water. When water flows, it takes the path of least resistance, and people are the same way. We tend to gravitate to tasks that require the least amount of energy from us. That is why passive hobbies, like watching television, are so popular. We do not have to do anything to get that information into our heads. Just sit, passively, and watch the screen, and the show's producers will tell us everything we need to know.

When it comes to dealing with the criminal element, it is important to understand this quirk about human nature. Most will take the path of least resistance, the easier target. An unlocked house is an easier target than a locked one. A locked house that is obviously unoccupied is an easier target than a house with someone in it. A locked house with flimsy doors is an easier target than a locked house with steel doors. The point is that the more obstacles a potential attacker or thief has to overcome, the less willing he may be to attempt breaking in.

At some point, neighborhoods will want to permanently block the easy entrances, places where vehicles or large groups of people can easily get into the neighborhood. Those fabulous SUVs that will be useless without cheap gasoline will be a good choice for a blockade, being careful to siphon any gasoline in the tank for use in generators. Felling trees across roadways is also a good option.

But since the collapse is still a day or two away, and we are still really only concentrating on what we can personally accomplish, the question is what can we do today to create more obstacles on our personal property, and the first choice should be a fence. Almost any fence is better than none. It not only defines boundaries for livestock, pets and children, but climbing a fence is more difficult than sauntering boldly across a yard up to the door. A good, sturdy wooden fence with a large-sounding dog on the other side would serve as a good deterrent.

Strategic plantings can also be crime deterrents. Since we are using edible plants for all of our landscaping and trying to make the most of our space, berry brambles planted under windows would keep all but the most tenacious criminals out. We might also consider some stronger window coverings. Blinds are pretty, but would not do much if someone on the outside broke my window. Solid wooden shutters, affixed to the inside of the window with a sturdy latching mechanism would prevent most people from getting in, and they have an added bonus. The shutters would provide further insulation at night when the temperatures are colder, and if heating our houses is an issue, any way we can keep the cold air out and the warm air in is a bonus.

A steel-core door with a dead-bolt lock is probably the best option, and if one has the money to replace the door, now would be a good time to do so. However, most inward-opening doors, regardless of the construction, can be kicked in with a well-placed heel. The door will hold, in most cases, but the frame often does not. There are two options to remedy this. Back in the pioneer days, a bar would be placed across the door at night and during times of trouble. Kicking in a door with this mechanism would be very difficult. Most hardware stores sell them for as little as $20.

A second option is to create a visible barrier outside the main door. Many homes already have storm doors. Usually these are an aluminum frame with a glass or screen insert. Since I have dogs and my primary reason for wanting a storm or screen door is to leave the main door open during the summer, my screen door would have to be reinforced with vertical rods from the top of the frame to the bottom. This construction and dead-bolt locks would make it more difficult to just break through my main door.

If the best defense is a good offense, the best thing we can do is to make our homes look as undesirable a mark as possible, and one way to do that is to throw up as many barriers as we can find.

Most of the people who talk about the coming collapse believe that the result will be widespread and violent civil unrest. The extent of what most of us experience will really depend on where we live, and while I do not advocate curling up in a ball and hoping it all away, nor running to the sporting goods store and buying one each of every gun in stock and enough rounds for a small platoon, I do recommend becoming more aware of the possibility and taking some steps to protect oneself. The best protection will always be to make oneself seem less desirable a mark. In short, do not be an easy target, and put up as many barriers between harm and self as possible.

We have one day left. If you do not feel safe, you probably are not, but you could be with just a little effort.

# DAY 21

# Transportation

I am a product of the audio/video age. In fact, anyone born after 1960 grew up with a television in the house and a favorite seat at the movie theatre. One of the greatest inventions of our time was the ability to buy and watch full-length feature films in the privacy of our homes, and I do not know anyone who does not have a few DVDs and a subscription to Netflix, a favorite Red Box location or a membership at a local video store.

Because I grew up watching movies and televisions, a lot of the visual references in my brain are from movies. One of my favorites will always be *Fiddler on the Roof*. I just love the opening scene where Tevye is delivering milk and cheese to his neighbors. He sings "Tradition. Tradition!" His mode of transportation is a wagon pulled by a horse.

While my young daughters would love nothing more than for us to get a horse, we have a quarter of an acre, like most suburbanites. With no garage and no place to build a barn, we can not

provide adequate shelter for a horse. Further, with only a quarter of an acre, there is not much room for our horse to graze. My
neighbors might be amenable to us grazing our horse on their
lawns, provided we clean up the droppings, but if the whole neighborhood needs to be devoted to food production, having a horse is
a poor use of the land.

If we are to lose our cars, however, we will need to find some
other way to get around. The obvious and cheapest choice is our
own two feet. Walking requires no special equipment, no skills or
knowledge. Most of us were doing it before we could even control
our bowels, and the idea that special shoes are needed to protect
our feet and knee and hip joints is a myth perpetuated by a very
creative group of marketing professionals and some eager foot-
wear manufacturers. Research suggests that shoes are part of the
reason we have foot, knee, hip and back issues. The best shoes for
walking are socks, or rather shoes with a completely flexible sole
that works only to protect the feet from getting cut and does not
limit normal foot movements, like moccasins.

The average adult can easily walk a mile in about fifteen minutes, or four miles an hour. There was a time when I walked four
miles to go shopping and walked four miles to get back home with
my purchases. My shopping trips took about three hours. Now, I
drive five miles through highly congested areas, often where construction is stalling traffic, through numerous traffic lights and in
the midst of people who, based on their driving skill/habits, must
be either suicidal or homicidal, and, as a result, my shopping trips
seem to take the same amount of time. Back when I was walking
to the store, I got infinitely more exercise, fresh air and sunshine
and was more relaxed than now, when I have to drive. The difference is that then I was alone and shopping only for myself, which
means I could walk at a much faster sustained pace than I can now,
with children walking along with me.

In addition, before I had children, I did not buy as much, and so carrying my purchases home was never an issue. The problem with walking being the primary means of transportation is getting stuff back, and the carrying capacity of a human being is pretty limited. In college, I didn't have a car, and we would occasionally bring our groceries home in the grocery cart, which could be construed as stealing (although we always took the carts back to the store, later).

Of course, in a lower-energy society, we will not need to push a cartload of groceries home, but we may need to bring home bundles of fire wood, or bags of animal feed, or pumpkins or apples from the local farmer, or any number of other items that are heavy, bulky or awkward to carry. The problem is that my local farmer does not have any grocery carts, and I would never suggest that we all take one now, while we can, and stash it in the garage until we need it. That would be stealing. Besides, there are alternatives to trying to lug home a bushel of apples in bags or sinking to stealing shopping carts.

The first option is a wagon, something many of us probably already have. I have three. Two of them are plastic kids' wagons and are old and the wheels don't turn well, but they still work, and with a little imagination, we could probably fix the wheels. The other is a garden cart, which is great for hauling all sorts of heavy things, including wood…and children.

Personally, however, I do not enjoy pulling a wagon for long distances. Just the ergonomics of the way one walks while pulling a wagon is uncomfortable and for long distances, if a wagon were how I transported stuff, I would want to design a harness that I could attach to myself, instead of trying to pull the wagon five miles using the handle. It would look funny, but it would be a better option, and it would keep my hands free for scratching or swatting bugs.

As long as I am thinking about harnesses, though, I would probably want to consider having someone or something else to pull my wagon. I already know that a horse, the traditional draft animal, is out of the question, because of space restrictions, but there are smaller animals, who would do well for pulling light loads, and anything I could pull, they could pull...probably better.

My first choice would be a goat. I am all about multi-use. We have chickens for eggs, fertilizer and meat, and rabbits for fertilizer and meat, and ducks for eggs, bug control and meat. A goat would be useful as a lawnmower, for milk (and cheese as a by-product of the milk), for meat and as a draft animal for pulling a lightweight cart, like one of our wagons. Goat pellets also make good fertilizer, and small goats are ideal as suburban livestock. The problem is that a small goat, which is best for suburban livestock, might be too small for use as a draft animal, and a larger goat might be too large for the suburban farm.

With the ideal being multi-use for small spaces, the next best option for a suburban draft animal is a dog. Historically, dogs were often used as draft animals, because they were cheaper to keep than horses, and it is only in our modern suburbs where a dog's function is purely as a companion animal. Dogs like to have a purpose, and there are many breeds of dog that are happier with a job. Any of the giant breeds of dogs would be useful for pulling loads, but the Bernese Mountain dog, Greater Swiss Mountain dog, Mastiff and Newfoundland are breeds that have a history of being used as draft animals.

In addition to all of the great arguments for having large dogs, HOA restrictions rarely limit dogs, regardless of their size, and so even if one lives in a place where goats and horses would be prohibited (not that we're going to worry too much about that, because we're going to get the restrictions changed, right?), one could still have a dog to pull the cart with no legal problems from the neighbors.

With the idea of multi-function in mind, though, a dog is also a great choice because a big dog is often a crime deterrent as was discussed previously. Further, many of the larger dog breeds were originally used as herd dogs for protecting and directing livestock. In suburban family life, these furry, four-legged shepherds will often view their humans as the "flock," and if danger is present, their natural protective instincts will kick in.

And if that is not convincing enough, dogs also make good bed warmers. In a lower-energy future where central heating will likely be a thing of the past, having that extra body heat can be very nice.

Unfortunately, while the dog would have little problem pulling a (small) wagon load of groceries home from the store, he will not be able to also pull the humans, which means walking alongside the dog and wagon. While four miles per hour is a good pace, it is still pretty slow, and there will be times when we might want to move a little faster or go a little further.

For low-energy wheeled transportation, most people would choose a bicycle, and for longer distance treks (more than four miles) a bike is a better choice than going on foot. With the addition of a cargo trailer, a regular bicycle can be a great way to transport goods. Trailers designed to transport people (specifically children) can also be used for carrying some types of cargo — like groceries... or that bushel of apples from the farm stand.

Some people do not want to pull a trailer, however, and an alternative is a cargo bike. There are a lot of really great options for cargo bikes. The Xtracycle or SUB (sport utility bike), which has gotten a lot of really positive press, allows the transport of all kinds of cargo from groceries to children. I have even seen a local fellow who transports his kayak down to the beach on his Xtracycle. A regular bike can be transformed into an Xtracycle with a kit sold on the Internet. With a trailer attached to an Xtracycle, a bike increases its ability to move whatever needs to be moved.

The best all-around bike for use as a primary means of transportation is a mountain bike, which unlike a road bike is built for durability instead of speed. In a lower-energy future, roads will unlikely be as well-maintained as they are now, and it is just as likely that our current, mostly unpaved, walking paths will become the highways once bicycles replace cars as the main mode of transportation. While mountain bikes perform best on rugged terrain, they are built to be functional on all surfaces and can be comfortably ridden on both blacktop and a dirt path, and can go easily from one to the other, which road bikes can not do.

Two-wheeled human-powered transportation does not have to be the only option. Quadricycles and/or pedicabs are also possible choices. Some even have enclosed passenger areas with under-the-seat storage so that passengers and cargo do not have to be exposed to the elements (being a passenger on a cycle in inclement weather can be uncomfortable). Teenager David Dixon of Novato,

California built a Solar Human Hybrid (SOHH) cycle that uses a solar panel mounted to a quadricycle (they used the ZEM manufactured in Switzerland) that gives an electric assist which allows a speed of 12 mph to 18 mph. The middle-schooler and his family state that the SOHH has replaced their car for in-town errands.

The only real drawback to cycles of any sort is the cost: a decent mountain bike starts at $120, and a pedicab starts at $3,000. The ZEM used in the SOHH was almost $4,000 (not including the cost of modifying the bike to make it solar powered).

Another concern further down the road for developing a dependence on bikes for transportation is the possibility that parts might become difficult to find, but my hunch is that we will not run out of salvageable materials for a pretty good long time, even after manufacturing replacement parts becomes a thing of the past.

Still, if I had to choose just one way to get around when I do not have my car anymore, I would pick the dog.

Whatever you decide, you should do it, today, because tomorrow…well, as Porky Pig is fond of saying, *That's all folks!*

(**Referenced article: Mack, Ben. Homemade Solar Quadricycle with Room for the Dog. Wired.com. June 8, 2009: wired.com/autopia/2009/06/homemade-solar.)

# DAY 22

# Afterword

American writer Will Durant observed, "A great civilization is not conquered from without until it has destroyed itself from within."

Our great global civilization had nowhere left to go. As we all learned when we were children and blowing up balloons, a thing can only get so big before it explodes, or like we learned with our first cake, it can only expand so far before it falls back into itself. Either way, it can only go so far, and the end result is never very pretty.

It happened. Like so many dominoes falling, as one system failed, the others quickly followed. A rise in the cost of oil resulted in a stalling of the transportation industry, which caused a slow in the shipping of goods from place to place. When sellers could not get their wares to buyers around the globe, economies began to fail, which caused widespread unemployment, resulting in no money to buy stuff and nothing much to buy, including food. Alternatives had to be found and quick.

The end was not pretty, and we were thankful, more than once, that we had started making changes sooner rather than later. It meant we spent the bulk of our disposable income on things like oil lanterns, apple trees and seeds, and that we never did get the chance to see some favorite television program on a 32" high-def television or discover what it was like to drive a truck with a hemi, but we have never *lived to regret* missing out on so much of what was our great American culture. Unfortunately, too many of our neighbors, friends and family did not live to regret not making changes quickly enough.

Of course, the one most important thing we learned was that, even in the midst of total collapse, life goes on. Such was the case for my neighborhood after the collapse. In fact, we should take a walk. Today is a very exciting day. There's going to be a wedding.

Right there, that first house on the left, that's the Cyr family's house. Back before the collapse, Mr. Cyr was the town fire chief. He's been working with the Lincoln boys to build masonry heaters and install woodstoves for those who were lucky enough to find them. Today, they're working on finishing the outdoor kitchen for Missy Harrison. It's her house where the wedding is taking place. She's a notary. Her husband, Jim, is a carpenter. He used to work piecing together factory-manufactured, modular homes. He does all sorts of carpentry work, from simple furniture pieces to the more elaborate wedding gazebo he's finishing up today. Missy decided that, since there wasn't a church in our neighborhood, perhaps turning her backyard into a wedding chapel would be useful. They're planning to convert their garage for use during the winter. That will probably be Jim's next project.

Smell that? Oh man, does that smell yummy! Joe Pierson must be cooking something scrumptious. He owned a restaurant back in the day, but now, he mostly bakes. The first project Mr. Cyr and his crew finished was the outdoor kitchen, complete with a masonry oven for Joe. Cake isn't much of a staple around here, as there isn't much in the way of sugar, but bread is still something we can enjoy, and it smells like Joe is making a maple bread of some sort. It's likely to be better than any wedding cake we ever had before.

Oh, look, there's Trevor Moss. He's delivering milk and cheese. Let's stop for a minute and pet Cujo. I don't know what possessed him to name his dog after that horrific character. Perhaps as a reminder that rabies is a real threat these days with vaccinations no longer standard. He's a good dog. Never a drop of milk spilled, and I hear he's really good at herding the cow down the road to the unfinished development. It was fortuitous, for us, that the owner kept the lots cleared and mowed. It makes a nice grazing area for the few large animals we were able to get for our community. It probably didn't hurt that we were so close to that huge dairy farm, either. When the power went off, milking 100 cows was impossible for the farmer, even with the help of his large family. He was happy to give us a cow.

Well, not *give*, exactly. We had to work out a barter system that was fair, and of course, it will be tweaked over time, but to start, we just took fair market value, as it was on day 21, right before the collapse, of the goods and services we had to offer. We each earn points based on our good or service, and we trade with each other using those points. Ms. Cratchitt was the local math teacher before the collapse, and she is now our community accountant…or banker. Whichever title she has adopted, she's the one that keeps track of how many points everyone has. There's only been one family who didn't like our system, and they moved. They deeded their house to our community before they left, and we made sure they had all of the supplies we could spare in hopes that their journey would be easier.

That's where Polly and Roy will live after their wedding.

Speaking of that, there's Polly now, heading over to Cecile's house. Cecile had a salon in town before the collapse. She has since moved her salon to her house. She's one of the few people who is still doing the same thing she did before the collapse. Well, except that she had to learn to cut hair without clippers, and she doesn't use chemicals anymore, which is probably better. She did mention at one point that her asthma seems to have cleared up a bit. It could be the lack of exposure to the chemicals she used in her profession; it could be something else. We may never know.

She also had to learn to shave using a straight razor, which was not terribly fun for her first few guinea pigs…er, customers, but once she got the hang of it, there have been very few men who don't go to her rather than try to wield the tool themselves. A couple of holdouts still have disposable razors, but in time, they will likely find her services valuable. Roy is one of the holdouts, although his skill at the forge is what keeps Cecile's razors and scissors, not to mention most of the other tools in the community shed, in working condition.

Roy was a college student before the collapse, studying software engineering. He always said that computers were just for money, but his passion was metallurgy, and if he could have thought of a way to make a living at blacksmithing, which he studied as a teenager, before the collapse, I believe he would never have gone to college. He's honed his skill over the years, and he was able to make the wedding bands for himself and Polly. She doesn't know. It's a surprise.

Their clothes are another surprise. Sally Weston has been altering clothes found in people's closets into more useful, more utilitarian and more durable pieces. She also makes special items, like Polly's dress. She repurposed bits and pieces of clothes into a stunning gown. Sally's creation put Scarlet O'Hara's green drapery makeover to shame.

Oh, watch your step! Trevor's son, Clarence, is taking the fatted calf up to Ken. Whether by fate or by design, Ken's house is at the end of the road, back along the edge of the woods, which is a good place for a butcher to live — kind of off the beaten path. Any of that typical, pre-collapse American squeamishness about where our food comes from is mostly a thing of the past, but if it doesn't have to be in our face, we'd just as soon it not be.

None of the cow will be wasted, and that's what's most important to us these days. The hide and head will go to Jack, our resident leathersmith, so that he can tan it. Bridget will take the fat and render it down into tallow and lard and make some candles. Some of it will be taken over to the Trading Post, where Ms. Cratchitt will make sure that those who need it for cooking can get it, for points, of course. The rest will be taken to Bonnie, who makes soap. She's gotten quite good, although most of us wouldn't know a good soap from a bad one, and she still claims to waste almost as much as is usable.

At first her soaps were just utilitarian, and we were clean, albeit not "clean" like the detergent clean most of us had become accustomed to being. It took a while to get used to not smelling "clean." When Jan's herbs started coming in strong, and Bonnie started adding some to her soaps, they really improved. Most folks like the peppermint soap for summer time, as it's cooling, and prefer the sage in the winter. A favorite was the time she was given some patchouli from a plant someone had bought at a local garden center before the collapse and kept alive in a pot. Patchouli is not native to our climate and would never grow outside. Unfortunately, the plant didn't last for very long, but it was fun to have the patchouli-scented soap while it was available.

It was lucky for us that most of the neighborhood heeded the warnings and set up water collection/storage systems or dug wells before the collapse. Most houses no longer have indoor running water, but nearly everyone has something for water storage outside, and there are plenty of buckets for hauling water into the house. Dave Branson is working on the plumbing issue, and there's even talk of building a water tower, but right now, most folks just carry water into the house.

We were very lucky to live in a neighborhood where we all had a septic system, rather than a sewer system. Since carrying water into the house is such a chore, no one really wants to waste it flushing the toilet, and so most folks just use a bucket in the house and empty the bucket into the septic tank, which has actually made the idea of composting humanure a more acceptable option. Most of us agreed that if we have to carry it outside, anyway, what's the difference between dumping it into the existing septic tank or dumping it into a composting barrel?

The good news is that we all have water, and no one has decided to build an old-fashioned (and not terribly sanitary) outhouse with a latrine trench (yet).

With regard to the water situation, there have been some very clever modifications. For instance, Cecile needed hot water in her salon, and so she and Dave cobbled together a solar water heater that sits on the roof of their garage. They put a hole in the roof and threaded a hose right into the salon from the water heater so that she can wash hair. The water isn't as hot as what most of us used to think of as "hot" water, but it's better than washing hair with cold water, or trying to heat water on the fire outside or on the woodstove (for those who have them). A few other people have set up outdoor solar showers, but of course, in our climate, they are only good for a few months out of the year. Dave is talking about building a wood-fired hot tub in his shed outside for use during the winter. If he does, I'm sure he will have a lot of visitors anxious for a hot bath. There's just nothing quite as wonderful as feeling clean.

You might not want to take too big a whiff near this house. Hans lives here with his wife and son. They moved over after the collapse, taking the chance on squatting in one of the too many foreclosed and empty houses. Hans has all sorts of information about squatting laws, and apparently, there is some obscure law that allows people to take possession of abandoned property. The bottom line is that the bank will probably never come this way again and likely cares less about this neighborhood, but the fact is that with Hans and Lisa living there, they're actually making sure the house is maintained in livable condition. If anything, the bank owes them a favor.

Hans is an old friend of ours from before the collapse, and we were thrilled when he ended up in our neck of the woods, so to speak. Plus, he brought with him a very valuable skill and has been putting it to good use. Very few of our community members haven't enjoyed his creations, and those were mostly the youngest members. He's been fermenting a special batch of honey for this special day. He says that, back in medieval times, mead was the wedding drink, and it is the source of the term "honeymoon." He's hoping his mead will provide the right atmosphere for our newest couple as they start their lives together.

Dale, our community gardener, helped Hans with planting hops, too, and so Hans has been experimenting with different beer recipes. That's the smell. Sometimes brewing doesn't give off the most pleasant aroma.

Speaking of the gardens, Dale has done an amazing job of helping people transition from their lawns to edible landscapes. He maintains most of the larger community gardens, especially those that are on the lawns of vacant houses, but most of us have our own kitchen gardens. Most of the neighborhood landscape design is based on permaculture techniques. Dale says, at some point, he's going to put himself out of work, but in addition to doing most of the planting and landscaping, Dale and his wife also work very hard at teaching the rest of us how to use some of the less familiar food growing in our area—like acorns.

What's that? My house? It's over there, across the way. Yeah, we could have moved into one of these big empty places. Lots of them emptied pretty quickly, but we already had everything we needed over there. We had spent a lot of time and energy prior to the collapse on building self-sufficiency into our lives, and so we already had our gardens, our rainwater reclamation system, our woodstove with a cook top, our outdoor kitchen and our animals, including the bees. It just seemed like a lot more trouble to move than was necessary. Most of our neighbors were gone right after the collapse, but we're keeping their properties maintained, and when it's time, we figure our girls can take their pick.

Our location makes it perfect, though, for our jobs. Using one of the outbuildings on our neighbor's property, I made a small library. Most of the books are ones I have collected over several decades of being a book hoarder. For once, my pack-rat tendencies have proven valuable. I had quite an impressive collection of both old and new, fiction and non-fiction, in every genre, and even in other languages. Books have always been my passion, and it was an obvious choice for me to be the keeper of the word, as it were.

Dem set up a small clinic in one of the other outbuildings on our neighbor's property. He is the midwife and community healer. We have Doc, who is good for patching up, and we have Dem, who is good for curing. It might seem odd to have a man serve in a midwifery role, but two things made him the best choice for our community. First was that he had just finished his training in herbalism and healing, and second was that he was the only person in our neighborhood who had delivered a baby before. The irony is that it never had occurred to either of us that this would be his calling, and we probably would never have started down the path if it hadn't been for Hans's wife having a baby in those early days and needing some help. They knew that he'd delivered our youngest and with nowhere else to turn, came to us. The rest, as they say, is history.

What's that? School? We don't really have an organized school. All kids are taught to read, usually by their parents, and our community library is a very busy place, all of the time. At the moment, everyone is home-schooled, although some parents will trade childcare responsibilities with other parents, when they need to do something, or need a break. Older kids have the option of being an apprentice. Joe already has two apprentices, which is good, because he needed the help. I already mentioned Mr. Cyr working with the Lincoln boys, and Jim is training my daughter and her friend. All of the kids who haven't chosen a specific apprenticeship help Dale with making the gardens or help Trevor with the cows.

A few of the kids have started a community paper to keep everyone up on what's happening, but we're concerned about paper becoming scarce. We'll probably end up with some other option for spreading the word. So far, we've been able to trade some things with other communities, but our resources are pretty limited, and with our 30 families to feed and care for, we just don't have a lot to spare.

We should head back over to Missy's place. The wedding will be taking place soon. Everyone will be there, and we'll have lots of great food. There's no caterer, but everyone will bring something to share. We'll also have music and dancing. We were lucky to have a professional musician in our neighborhood before the collapse, and he'll provide some tunes. Some of the kids have been taking lessons from him in the evenings, too, and they'll play some pieces they've prepared. Good company, good food, good music, and....

"Oh, hi, Hans! Need some help with that?"

# Bibliography

Brown, Tom. *Field Guide to Living with the Earth*. Berkley Books, 1984.

Bubel, Mike & Nancy. *Root Cellaring* . Storey Publishing ( Versa Press), 1991.

Chevallier, Andrew. *The Encyclopedia of Medicinal Plants*. D.K. Publishing, 1996.

Crawford, Martin. *Creating a Forest Garden*. Green Books, 2010.

Egan, Timothy. *The Worst Hard Times*. Houghton Mifflin, 2006.

Emery, Carla. *The Encyclopedia of Country Living*, 10th ed. Sasquatch Books, 2008.

Halacy, Beth & Dan. *Cooking with the Sun*. Morning Sun Press, 1992.

Hupping, Carol (& the Staff of the Rodale Food Center). *Stocking Up*. Simon and Schuster, 1986.

Jenkins, Joseph. *Humanure*. Joseph Jenkins, Inc., 2005.

Kilarski, Barbara. *Keep Chickens*. Storey Publishing, 2003.

Mack, Ben. "Homemade Solar Quadricycle with Room for the Dog." Wired.com, June 8, 2009: wired.com/autopia/2009/06/homemade-solar.

Nearing, Scott & Helen. *The Good Life*. Schocken Books, 1989.

Orlov, Dmitry. *Reinventing Collapse*. New Society Publishers, 2008.

Pollan, Michael. *Omnivore's Dilemma*. Penguin Group, 2006.

Thayer, Samuel. *The Forager's Harvest*. Forager's Harvest, 2006.

Thayer, Samuel. *Nature's Garden*. Forager's Harvest, 2010.

Werner, David. *Where There Is No Doctor*, Hesperian Press, 1977.

Online resources:

American Library Association's Most Challenged Books list: ala.org/ala/issuesadvocacy/banned/frequentlychallenged/challengedclassics/index.cfm)

Colonial Soap-making: alcasoft.com/soapfact/history.html

Freecycle: freecycle.org

Lye-making: lifeunplugged.net/everythingelse/make-lye-from-wood-ash.aspx

Statistics on school buildings: edfacilities.org/ds/statistics.cfm#

# Index

# About the Author

**WENDY BROWN** earned a B.A. in English from Eastern Kentucky University in 1989, and immediately began pursuing a graduate-level degree in creative writing when the need to earn a living superseded her desire for further education, and she took a job teaching English at a rural school in a tiny northern Kentucky county. Wendy's career path took a sharp left turn from there, and since then, she has worked as a restaurant manager, enlisted in the US Army, and started a home-based business. She has now come full circle and reacquainted herself with her first love, writing. Wendy has published articles on several ezines and writes regularly on her blog at happilyhome.blogspot.com, where she talks about life, liberty, and the pursuit of homesteading on a quarter acre. She lives with her amazing husband, their three beautiful daughters, eight chickens, four rabbits, three ducks, two dogs, and an abnormally large, black cat named Mr. Pumpkin in the suburbs of southern Maine.

If you have enjoyed *Surviving the Apocalypse in the Suburbs,*
you might also enjoy other

# BOOKS TO BUILD A NEW SOCIETY

Our books provide positive solutions for people who want
to make a difference. We specialize in:

Sustainable Living • Green Building • Peak Oil • Renewable Energy
Environment & Economy • Natural Building & Appropriate Technology
Progressive Leadership • Resistance and Community
Educational and Parenting Resources

## New Society Publishers

### ENVIRONMENTAL BENEFITS STATEMENT

New Society Publishers has chosen to produce this book on recycled
paper made with 100% post consumer waste, processed chlorine free,
and old growth free.

For every 5,000 books printed, New Society Publishers saves the
following resources:[1]

| | |
|---|---|
| 42 | Trees |
| 3,805 | Pounds of Solid Waste |
| 4,186 | Gallons of Water |
| 5,460 | Kilowatt Hours of Electricity |
| 6,916 | Pounds of Greenhouse Gases |
| 30 | Pounds of HAPs, VOCs, and AOX Combined |
| 11 | Cubic Yards of Landfill Space |

[1]Environmental benefits are calculated based on research done by the Environmental
Defense Fund and the other members of the Paper Task Force who studied the
environmental impacts of the paper industry.

For a full list of NSP's titles, please call 1-800-567-6772
or check out our website at: www.newsociety.com

NEW SOCIETY PUBLISHERS
www.newsociety.com